God Invites You to Enjoy

The Pleasure of His Company

JUDY WARPOLE

WestBow
PRESS
A DIVISION OF THOMAS NELSON

WestBow Press books may be ordered through booksellers or by contacting:

WestBow Press
A Division of Thomas Nelson
1663 Liberty Drive
Bloomington, IN 47403
www.westbowpress.com
1-(866) 928-1240

Because of the dynamic nature of the Internet, any web addresses or links contained in
this book may have changed since publication and may no longer be valid. The views
expressed in this work are solely those of the author and do not necessarily reflect the views
of the publisher, and the publisher hereby disclaims any responsibility for them.

Any people depicted in stock imagery provided by Thinkstock are models,
and such images are being used for illustrative purposes only.

Certain stock imagery © Thinkstock.

ISBN: 978-1-4497-9913-7 (sc)
ISBN: 978-1-4497-9912-0 (hc)
ISBN: 978-1-4497-9914-4 (e)

Library of Congress Control Number: 2013913637

Printed in the United States of America.

WestBow Press rev. date: 7/25/2013

*To Ron, my husband and best friend,
my encourager!*

I thank God for you!

Contents

Preface

The Pleasure of His Company came from a deep longing for a closer relationship with Jesus and moment-by-moment awareness of the presence of God. While searching for healing and renewal during a season of many disappointments, I found everything I needed in the comfort of Jesus. I was advised to visualize putting all my cares and concerns into a basket and laying them at Jesus' feet. I did just that. I let my soul and mind rest.

What I discovered for myself has overflowed to those who have come into my circle of love and ministry.

In 1992 my husband Ron and I flew to Moscow, Russia, and then onto Rostov-on-Don—750 miles further south—where we were to live and share our lives with a small group of new Christians. These precious ones were the first of many who opened their hearts and lives to the One who is guiding their journey to heaven. This small body of believers grew daily in number as Jesus added to His church in that place. They also began to grow in God's wisdom as they were reading God's Word for the first time in their lives. Ron and I were teaching day and night, from house to house including hours of daily classes in our small, Soviet-style, fourth floor walk-up apartment.

As I sat at our tiny kitchen table listening to these new babes, it was not long until many began to ask how to pray to God and how to have the personal relationship they were hearing about.

Motivated because of their requests, I began to prepare outlines for a practical prayer guide. I taught the women one-on-one as well as the group who met together on Tuesday nights in what had formerly been a Communist assembly hall.

Four years later, when a dear Russian brother was ready to assume his role as pulpit preacher and teacher, my husband and I prepared to move to Tallinn, the capital city of Estonia. Another small group of new Christians had requested someone come to help them learn how to lead others to Christ and how to mature their growing church family.

Before we moved to Tallinn, the ladies in Rostov-on-Don, after four years of growing in the Lord, asked me to re-teach the lessons on prayer. They said, "We need to renew our commitment to prayer. We know we have matured and that we will relate to the lessons in a different way than we did four years ago. So, please teach us again." So I taught once again what would one day become the book in your hands.

Then we went to work with the church in Tallinn, the lessons were taught … and taught again a few years later … and taught again a few years after that. After twelve of what would be our fifteen years in Tallinn and four overlapping years in Estonia's university city of Tartu, the Christians suggested that I teach it yet again. This time the request came with even greater responsibility because one of the women—a published writer—challenged me to write chapters instead of newly revised outlines for the lessons. I accepted the challenge.

As I wrote each chapter, I emailed it to our dear friends Ray and Susan Wilson, who read each chapter and encouraged me to keep writing. When *"the book"* was finished, Ray prepared a questionnaire to accompany the manuscript. He asked several of the members of the church to read and critique. To this day I thank God for each of these dear people and their suggestions and encouragement.

The manuscript lay dormant for several years because the idea of publishing and reading the words "No unsolicited manuscripts will be accepted" intimidated me. Until ... January 2013 when I found a two-year old email from Ray with a link to WestBow Press. I prayed asking God, "Is this *the* time?" Mordicai's words to Esther rang in my ears, "Maybe thou art come to the kingdom for such a time as this."

My desire is that these lessons will be used to remind us of many things we may already know. For a new Christian, may you draw nearer to God and grow in Him as you read. The lessons are devotional, inspirational and worded in such a way that God's written thoughts and instructions create an interactive communication.

There are thirteen chapters. *The Invitation* is to be used with Chapter 1. The thirteen chapters can also be used for a quarterly series.

At the very end you will see a two-sided Prayer Guide Outline that you might want to copy or remove to keep in your Bible or with your Journal.

May God bless your reading!

To All of Us

Psalm 19:1-4

Dear One, I just had to write to tell you how much I love you and care for you. Yesterday, I saw you walking and laughing with your friends. I hoped that soon you would want Me to walk along with you. So, I painted you a sunset to close your day and whispered a soft breeze to refresh you.

As I watched you fall asleep last night, I spilled moonlight onto your face--on your cheeks where so many tears have been. You fell asleep and didn't even think of Me.

This morning I painted another beautiful sky for you. But you woke up late and rushed off. You didn't even notice.

I love you. If you would only listen, you'd know that I really love you. I try to say it in the quiet of the green grass of summer and in the blue of the sky. The wind whispers My love through the trees and paints beautiful colors in the fall leaves and in the springtime flowers. I shout it to you in the thunder of the waves on the seashore. And I compose love songs for birds to sing for you. I warm you with the clothing of sunshine and perfume the air with fresh snow. My love for you is deeper than any ocean and greater than any need in your heart.

My Father sends His love. I want you to spend time with Him and get to know Him better. I invite you to enjoy the pleasure of His company on earth as it is in heaven. So, please, accept His invitation. He will be waiting to hear from you!

Your brother and friend,
Jesus

RSVP

The Invitation

> "Come to me... learn from me...
> and you will find rest for your souls."
> Matthew 11:28-29 ESV

J esus continually invited His hearers to come. Come to Him. Come to His Father. Come because we are blessed by His Father (Matthew 25:34). Come and share in His happiness (Matthew 25:21, 23).

Jesus invited His hearers to listen and learn, promising wonderful blessings when His words are put into practice (Luke 8:21).

Jesus knew then, and He knows now that the demands of our daily lives, plus our responsibilities toward the people we love, plus the problems that challenge as well as the challenges that invigorate us, can be exhausting. And so, we hear Jesus, the embodiment of perfect wisdom and compassion, saying:

> "Come with me by yourselves
> to a quiet place and get some rest."
> Mark 6:31 NIV

Jesus invites us daily to a quiet place where we might receive much needed rest. This quiet place is found in the pleasure of our Father's company where we fix our thoughts on Jesus (Hebrews 3:1). It is the place where in Jesus and through faith in Him we may approach God freely and with confidence (Ephesians 3:12). It's the place where "the Lord takes pleasure in his people" (Psalm 149:4 ESV). It's the place where God takes delight in us!

In our hearts we hear His invitation to pray more than simple, brief prayers throughout the day. Chatting with the Lord throughout our day is good, but there may be a desire within us to spend longer periods of time with our God and Savior. Sometimes we want to embrace His call to prayer, but do not. Other times we do accept the invitation to spend an extended time in prayer, but we become frustrated and discouraged because our efforts to concentrate are undisciplined. We are so easily distracted. We cannot seem to focus our thoughts in meaningful uninterrupted communication.

The purpose of this book is to motivate and help equip each one of us to become more disciplined in prayer. The book brings together many Scriptures from God's Word that will remind you and teach you to pray with greater focus.

There are step-by-step reminders and instructions to help you maintain focus and actually pray with deeper and more meaningful words. As you hear His words of invitation and respond, you will affirm to your Heavenly Father that you desire the blessings Jesus promised when He said, "Blessed are those who hear the teaching of God and obey it" (Luke 11:28 NCV).

The practical reward of reading each chapter in this book and following each step will be the strengthening of your trust in

God's promise which states, "For the moment all discipline seems painful, but later on it yields the peaceful fruit of righteousness to those who have been trained by it." In the reading and doing, each one of us will, "strengthen our drooping hands and weak knees" (Hebrews 12:11-12 ESV).

And so, may we all say with the psalmist, "My heart has heard you say, 'Come and talk with me.' My heart responds, 'Lord I am coming'" (Psalm 27:8 NLT).

Chapter 1

The Pleasure of His Company

Realizing the delight that comes from being with God

> "You make known to me
> the path of life:
> You will fill me with joy
> in your presence,
> with eternal pleasures
> at your right hand."
>
> Psalm 16:11 NIV

Eternal pleasures! Joy in the presence of our Father! Everlasting contentment and fulfillment! Satisfaction! The invitation to enjoy the pleasures of God's company has already been accepted by many of us. For others, God is still waiting for a reply to His RSVP (French: *Respondez s'il vous plait*, "please respond"). Some in today's world are still awaiting the arrival of their personal invitation—an invitation they don't even know is addressed to them. And, sadly, others have declined His invitation, preferring to find their pleasure away from His presence.

This book is not about those who decline His invitation. This book is about the realization of pleasure that comes with the acceptance of His invitation. We will be reminded of the joy and thrill that is ours because God has seated us at His right hand. As more is learned about God, His Son Jesus, and the relationship they share, and our place in that relationship, the path of life—on earth and into heaven—will become clearer. God's path of life will lead us into an ever-deepening relationship with Him. Along this path of life the thrill of discovering that Jesus has given us everything we need to live and serve God (2 Peter 1:3) will delight each one of us who has heard His call and accepted His invitation.

As we listen to news on television and radio and read newspapers—hearing of war, crime, disaster and suffering, terrorists and tragedies, broken families and broken children—we worry and fret, wondering if there is anything good anywhere. Contrary to our longing for peace and security, we carry the burden of concern in our minds and emotions. Negative and fearful, surrounded by turmoil and anxiety, we struggle to hold onto our hopes as well as maintain a positive outlook on life.

Troubling thoughts can often plague us. Feeling distressed and powerless, we wonder what will happen next. Our nerves fray. Our hearts beat faster. We fret. We're easily annoyed. We brood and worry.

However, our caring God graciously offers us a better way to think, a way to trust, a way to be still and calm in the midst of a very uncertain world. Our Heavenly Father desires to fill us with joy in the pleasure of His company. He desires to enjoy the pleasure of *our* company. He invites us to take steps toward a deeper closeness with Him.

"Do not fret because of evildoers,
nor be envious of the workers of iniquity.
for they shall soon be cut down like the grass,
and wither as the green herb.
Trust in the LORD, and do good;
dwell in the land, and feed on His faithfulness.
Delight yourself also in the LORD,
and He shall give you the desires of your heart."

Psalm 37:1-4 NKJV

"Delight yourself in the Lord," precious words written as an imperative command revealing the path leading toward genuine hope and joy in a harsh and cruel world. When evil is everywhere, when power and corruption succeed over righteousness, comfort can be found in the inspired words David the psalmist wrote to encourage not only himself but all who would read his words. True pleasure is found in the company of the living God.

"Delight" is a word to ponder and meditate upon, a word whose meaning we know when we read it or hear it spoken; but if asked to define it and apply it personally, we struggle to find the precise words. Somehow, it has the sound of intimacy. It enters our minds as a gentle word, embracing our thoughts tenderly. We instinctively understand that delight is better than happy. It is more than joy. It is more than cheerfulness. Delight implies a completeness of body, soul, and spirit! Delight is wonderful, comfortable pleasure for God and for me. Delight is pleasure in the presence of one another's company!

People have always looked for pleasure, but not all find their pleasure in the company of God. The apostle Paul wrote about those who would seek their pleasure away from the presence of God:

> "Remember this! In the last days there will be many troubles, because people will love themselves, love money, brag, and be proud. They will say evil things against others and will not obey their parents or be thankful or be the kind of people God wants. They will not love others, will refuse to forgive, will gossip, and will not control themselves. They will be cruel, will hate what is good, will turn against their friends, and will do foolish things without thinking. They will be conceited, will love pleasure instead of God, and will act as if they serve God but will not have his power"
> (2 Timothy 3:1-5a NCV).

This selfish hardness of heart permeated the thinking of mankind back then, and it has continued into our time and will continue as long as time lasts. Hardness is all around us, robbing us of the true joys of life. Oftentimes, this hardness affects our lives even in relationships with our own family members whose love we need and cherish the most.

But, in the midst of the most disappointing and discouraging of circumstances and relationships, our Heavenly Father tells us where He finds His delight. He "delights in those who fear him, who put their hope in his unfailing love" (Psalm 147:11 NIV).

His delight and ours will be found as we share eternal pleasures:

"For the Lord takes delight in his people; he
crowns the humble with victory. Let his faithful
people rejoice in this honor and sing for joy..."
(Psalm 149:4-5 NIV).

Our Heavenly Father loves to give gifts to His children
(Matthew 7:11; Luke 11:1)! He desires to "satisfy our desires with
good things" (Psalm 103:5 NIV). He wants us to have the desires
of our hearts! He wants us to enjoy being with Him! Feeling
loved! Protected! Feeling safe! Fulfilled! Content! Happy!

Job—a righteous man in the eyes of God—suffered for a time.
He grieved the loss of his children. He was alone in his marriage
because his wife did not understand his faith nor did she share
his trust in God. Job was physically ill, unable to change his
circumstances, and misjudged by his friends. Yet, from the
words of one of his friends—albeit a friend who did not fully
understand the reason for Job's suffering—comes truth. The
words spoken by Job's friend are an ancient, but eternal guide
with steps toward finding pleasure in God's company. Steps
are revealed that bring us into a deeper relationship with God
where He hears our prayers and promises to help us. These
steps are in complete harmony with all other revealed thoughts
from our Heavenly Father. Each one of us may take these steps
toward delighting ourselves in the Lord.

Thoughtfully and with resolve, may we proceed from one step
of obedience to the next, letting each step take us into the
pleasure of His company:

"Yield now and be at peace with Him,
thereby good will come to you.

> Please receive instruction from His mouth
> and establish His words in your heart.
> If you return to the Almighty, you will be restored.
> If you remove unrighteousness far from your tent,
> … then you will delight in the Almighty
> and lift up your face to God.
> You will pray to Him, and He will hear you
> … and light will shine on your ways."
> Job 22:21-23, 26-28 NASB

Imagine a large auditorium filled with people. The speaker steps to the microphone and asks a simple question requiring the raising of hands: "How many feel your prayer life is what you want it to be?" In all probability, very few hands would be raised.

If the question were to be rephrased: "How many desire to have a closer relationship with God through prayer?" hands would be raised all around the room.

Let us hear ourselves responding in a very practical way to the advice given to Job:

> A deeper sense of God's presence!
> "Yes, I want that," we say.
> Trust in God to hear and understand
> the longings of my heart!
> "Yes, please, I want that too."
> Comfort as I wait for God to work out my problems!
> "Yes, this too."
> Take the first step: Yield to God!
> Take the second step: Receive instruction!

Take another step: Return to God!
Take another step: Remove sin!
Delight in the Almighty is found!
He hears my prayers!
His light shines on my life!
He gives me the desires of my heart!
The pleasure of His company is mine!

God has always given purpose and promise to motivate us into a deeper relationship with Him. When we open our eyes to see and open our ears to hear, we also open our hearts and minds to find pleasure in Him. And when we do as He has asked, we experience joy in knowing that He will give us the desires of our hearts:

"The LORD is near to all who call on him,
to all who call on him in truth.
He fulfills the desire of those who fear him;
He also hears their cry and saves them."
Psalm 145:18-19 ESV

Our eternal and loving Father finds great pleasure in those who call out to Him, those who listen to His words and treasure their truth. He promises to fulfill the desires of those who cry to Him. He promises to hear our prayers. We are assured that we will have because we ask (James 4:2b).

When we ask, we must ask with the right motives so that what our heart desires will bring joy to the Father. Because we desire to find pleasure in the company of our God, the desires of our hearts will not be based on wrong motives, the kind of desires that are intended to be spent on our own pleasures (James 4:3).

Prayerfully read and think about each desire
on the following list of

Desires of my heart
that bring joy to the Father

Make each desire your own by telling God,
"My heart desires _____ "

Example: "My heart desires <u>integrity</u>."
"My heart desires to be <u>loyal to you</u>."

NOTE: Words underlined by author for emphasis

Desires of my heart
that bring joy to the Father

- "I know my God that you test the heart and are pleased with <u>integrity</u>... Keep this desire in the hearts of your people forever, and keep their hearts <u>loyal to you</u>." (1 Chronicles 29:17- 18 NIV)

- "May he give you the desire of your heart and make <u>all your plans succeed</u>." (Psalm 20:4 NIV)

- "Whoever of you loves life and desires <u>to see many good days</u>, keep your tongue from evil and your lips from speaking lies. Turn from evil and do good; seek peace and pursue it." (Psalm 34:12-14 NIV)

- "I desire <u>to do your will</u>, O my God...." (Psalm 40:8 NIV)

- "There is <u>nothing</u> on earth I desire <u>besides you</u>." (Psalm 73:25b ESV)

- "The Lord is near to all who call on him, to all who call on him in truth. He fulfills the desire of those who <u>fear him</u>; he also <u>hears their cry</u> and <u>saves them</u>. The Lord <u>preserves</u> all who love him, but all the wicked he will destroy." (Psalm 145:18-20 ESV)

- "Blessed is the one who finds <u>wisdom</u>, the one who gains <u>understanding</u> ... Nothing you desire can compare with her." (Proverbs 3:13,15 ESV)

- "<u>A good name</u> is to be more desired than great riches." (Proverbs 22:1 NASB)

- "...<u>your name and remembrance</u> are the desire of our soul. My soul yearns for you in the night; my spirit within me earnestly longs for you." (Isaiah 26:8-9 ESV)

- "I have the desire <u>to do what is right</u>...." (Romans 7:18 ESV)

- "...those who live in accordance with the Spirit have their minds set on <u>what the Spirit desires</u>." (Romans 8:5b NIV)

- "But earnestly desire <u>the greater gifts</u>... <u>faith, hope and love</u>...." (1 Corinthians 12:3 and 13:13 NASB)

- "...finish the work you started. Then your <u>doing will be equal to your wanting to do</u>. Give from what you have." (2 Corinthians 8:11 NCV)

- "For to me to live is Christ, and to die is gain. If I am to live in the flesh, that means <u>fruitful labor</u> for me. Yet which I shall choose I cannot tell. I am hard pressed between the two. My desire is to depart and <u>be with Christ,</u> for that is far better. But <u>to remain in the flesh</u> is more necessary on your account." (Philippians 1:21-24 ESV)

- "Pray for us, for we are sure that we have a clear conscience, desiring to <u>act honorably in all things</u>." (Hebrews 13:18 ESV)

JESUS is my GUIDE into the Pleasure of His Company

"Send forth your light and your truth,
let them guide me.
Let them bring me... to the place where you dwell.
I will go to the altar of God,
to God my joy and my delight!"
Psalm 43:3-4 NIV

The steps God has shown will bring us to the joy and delight found only in the pleasure of His company. As we continually say "Yes" to each step, we are encouraged in the knowledge that we do not step even one step alone. As our desire to come closer to the heavenly altar grows, our eternal God sends us a guide. We address our guide by many names. When we desire to be taken to the place where God dwells, we call our guide: 'Light' and 'Truth.'

Jesus, the one who said, "I am the way and the truth and the life. No one comes to the Father except through me" (John 14:6 ESV) is the only one who can guide us to the altar of God. Jesus is the only one who answers to the name "Truth". He is the only one called "the light of the world" (John 8:12 ESV). He is the only one who can shine on the path of life.

Wherever He guides us, we will never walk in darkness, but will have the "light of life" (John 8:12 ESV). We may walk safely and confidently as we follow our guide into the very presence of Our Heavenly Father.

Through the eyes of faith, together—Jesus and I—go to the throne of God with confidence (Hebrews 4:16). We go surrounded

in His pure light and walking in truth. We go into the presence
of Almighty God. And once there, joy and delight are ours.

We receive wonderful pleasure at the altar of God. In His
presence we may express our innermost thoughts and desires—
desires that we submit to Him in order to be molded by His will.
Desires that will give us "many good days" (Psalm 34:12 NIV).

Building a Relationship in
the Pleasure of His Company

? ASK YOURSELF ?

Is the DESIRE of my heart to find
my DELIGHT in God?

If the answer is "YES", claim this promise:

"The DESIRES of the DILIGENT are fully satisfied!"
(Proverbs 13:4 NIV)

An equation is now formed whose results equal
"Delight in the Lord."

DESIRE + DILIGENCE = DELIGHT

Diligence in finding pleasure with God will mean that daily
choices must be made. Priorities must be rearranged so that more
time can be spent with Him—more time in His Word listening
to Him, more time in prayer speaking to Him. The desire for

a closer relationship may be very strong; but if we do not add diligence to the equation, what we desire may dissolve into only good intentions. There must be constant steady effort.

Are you ready to deepen your relationship with the Father so that you might enjoy the pleasure of His company?

Diligently begin . . .

Chapter 2

Building a House of Prayer

Desire plus diligence builds a delightful prayer life

> "It is written,' he said to them,
> 'My house will be called a
> HOUSE OF PRAYER.'"
> Matthew 21:13 NIV

Wise is the person who builds on the firm foundation of the words and example of Jesus. Wise is the builder who digs down deep and lays their foundation of faith on rock (Luke 6:46-48), on the rock that is Jesus (1 Corinthians 10:4). Only a foolish person builds on sand with no foundation. When times of trouble come, personal philosophy and the things of this world are like a foundation of sand. What is built upon a foundation of sand will crumble in the presence of God. Only that which is built on the principles and revealed will of our Heavenly Father will last into eternity (Matthew 7:24-27). "For no one can lay any foundation other than the one already laid, which is Jesus Christ" (1 Corinthians 3:11 NIV).

Just as "the wise woman builds her house, but the foolish tears it down with her own hands" (Proverbs 14:1 NASB), each one of us either builds a place where God is welcome; or we destroy the beauty He intends and build a house with empty rooms where the pleasure of God's company cannot be enjoyed.

> "By wisdom a house is built,
> and through understanding it is established;
> through knowledge its rooms are filled
> with rare and beautiful treasures."
> Proverbs 24:3-4 NIV

If we are building our spiritual, eternal houses by wisdom, as we gain more understanding of God and His will for us, our house will be fully established and approved by God. As we arrange each room based on knowledge of Him, we will be decorating our lives with rare and beautiful treasures. God calls us into His glory and goodness (2 Peter 1:3). He calls to invite us to build with Him so that our delight and pleasure may grow deeper and more meaningful. God has given us everything we need to live and serve Him (2 Peter 1:3). He wants us to accept His gifts.

Our personal dwelling place—our very self, our inner being—can surely become a place of welcome to our wonderful Heavenly Father. Each house must be erected exclusively with God's building supplies—the wisdom, understanding, and knowledge that come only from Him. Our interior decor will consist of beautiful treasures, blessings given in response to the desires of our hearts, blessings from God who loves to give good gifts to those who build with Him.

As we build, we agree with God that whatever we have learned or received or heard or seen that comes from Him, we put it into daily practice. And, as always, when we follow every clear directive from the Master Builder, He blesses us with His promise that the God of peace will be with us (Philippians 4:9).

He who has become our wisdom and righteousness will be with us as we build our spiritual houses. We will not build alone. He will always build with us.

While we are building, there will be many others building. Many active builders will have their own personal houses in progress at the same time. Where there are many houses under various stages of construction, a spiritual housing development grows.

God—our Site Manager—helps each individual builder. He oversees all construction and lovingly joins us together into a community of believers. Building together, we are His house! Our neighborhood of individual, spiritual houses is filled with love and protected by the greatest of security plans: Jesus Christ, who is "faithful as a Son over God's house. And we are God's house, if we confidently maintain our hope" (Hebrews 3:6 NCV).

Upon the foundation of Jesus, each individual house is framed in purity, walled in prayer, and covered with a roof of praise! God's heavenly construction plan must be carefully and regularly consulted. He must be recognized as the Master Builder because, in truth, He is the builder of everything! (Hebrews 3:4)

Jesus is the Master Architect

We consult with Jesus, who is also the Master Architect, to be certain we understand where to begin. As sub-contractors working under the authority and direction of God, each one listens to the words of Jesus, "Suppose one of you wants to build.... Will he not first sit down and estimate the cost to see if he has enough money to complete it? For if he lays the foundation and is not able to finish it, everyone who sees it will ridicule him" (Luke 14:28 NIV).

Yes, there will be building costs—time invested in Bible reading and study, as well as the budgeted line item of time for regular prayer. And if anyone feels they lack what is required to begin building, there is an investor ready to help. "He will credit righteousness for us who believe in him" (Romans 4:24 NIV) so that we are adequately funded to build on the words and life of Jesus.

On that day so very long ago, when Jesus went into the temple, we read by word and action that He unrolled and presented the schematic for building a House of Prayer. His words and actions are the Master Plan, the progression of building procedures He laid out.

The Blueprint

From the Gospel of Matthew 21:12-16 NIV

It is a House of Purity!

"Jesus entered the temple area and drove out all who were buying and selling there. He overturned the tables of the money changers and the benches of those selling doves (v. 12).

It is a House of Prayer!

"'It is written,' he said to them, 'My house will be called a HOUSE OF PRAYER' but you are making it a 'den of robbers' (v. 13 emphasis by author).

It is a House of Healing!

"The blind and the lame came to him at the temple, and he healed them (v. 14).

It is a House of Praise!

"But when the chief priests and the teachers of the law saw the wonderful things he did and the children shouting in the temple area, 'Hosanna to the Son of David,' they were indignant (v. 15). 'Do you hear what these children are saying?' they asked him. 'Yes,' replied Jesus, 'have you never read, From the lips of children and infants you have ordained praise?'" (v. 16)

For those of us who desire to build onto or remodel and improve our own House of Prayer, it will always be a wise plan to examine carefully the present condition of what we have already built. If sin has cracked the walls of relationship with God, we must make repairs. Like the attitude and action of Jesus in the temple, zeal to drive out sin must energize us to move quickly and decisively. We overturn old habits. We clear our heads and hearts of all confusion. There may be things in our lives that are not necessarily wrong, but have become misplaced priorities robbing us of the joy of building our House of Prayer into something beautiful. Like the doves released from their cages, we give wing to whatever has kept us from spending time in prayer with our Heavenly Father.

Even as walls of prayer begin to shape our houses, we realize that during the building process daily cleanup will always be necessary. Bent nails, sawdust, and damaged materials can be likened to temptation, weakness, fear, and hopelessness which, like construction trash, can clutter our thoughts and our prayers. Impure thoughts and useless worry, like bent nails, must be gathered up and discarded. The sawdust of disappointment and discouragement must be swept away. Every day as each builder cleans their own building site, words of commitment and resolve can be spoken, "I *will* be God's House of Purity!"

Our words declaring our desire to be God's House of Purity are like a spiritual mop and broom so that we say with each swish of the mop and swing of the broom:

> "Wash me thoroughly from my iniquity and cleanse me from my sin.... Create in me a pure heart, O God, and renew a steadfast spirit within me." (Psalm 51:2, 10 ESV)

Trusting in His forgiveness and with renewed strength of spirit, each one of us will look at the prayer life we are building and say with boldness, "I *will* be God's House of Prayer!"

After Jesus had driven out sin and chaos, after He had spoken with great zeal saying, "My house will be called a house of prayer," the dust settled. In the calmness that followed, the blind and lame recognized His authority and power. The time was now theirs, and they came to Jesus for healing. In the same way, when each individual's spiritual house is clean and walled in prayer, the time will come to enjoy the pleasure of His company. In the quietness of our soul we will present our requests to God and His peace which goes beyond our understanding will begin its quiet work in our hearts and minds (Philippians 4:6-7).

Our own emotions and thoughts will begin to heal in the presence of God. As the healing begins in us, our thoughts may be turned to others who need spiritual and physical healing. Then with a heart open to Him, we again speak saying, "I *will* be God's House of Healing!"

With our eyes closed, relaxing in a clean, quiet House of Prayer, people and places will come like guests into our thoughts. We will visualize people we know—people for whom we feel great concern. Our thoughts and spiritual eyes will see people who are living their lives crippled in body or spirit. We will see those we know who are unseeing, unhearing and unresponsive to the words of God. We can now let thoughts of them visit us in our House of Prayer. This will be a wonderful opportunity to speak about them to God because the desire of our heart is that healing will come to each one just as it comes to us in the company of our Heavenly Father.

25

As we speak to God about many things, we remember that in our House of Prayer we don't do all the talking. True communication is shared and interactive. We will open our eyes and read from the pages of God's Word. His inspired advice from His written words will bring much needed understanding and healing. His words will encourage us as well as give us the right words to speak to those we know who themselves are in need of healing.

Our house is not finished until it has the roof that the Master Planner designed. While Jesus was healing the blind and lame, the children began to praise him. Their loud and enthusiastic voices covered everything like an unseen roof. There was delightful praise!

The roof over the House of Prayer that each one of us is building will be praise! With our own mouths each one will say, "I *will* be God's House of Praise!" We will hear ourselves speak resounding declarations as we build the House where we can enjoy the pleasure of His company. We hear and are strengthened.

Jesus responded, "Yes," when asked, "Do you hear what these children are saying?"

Hammers and saws that are used to build houses resound in the ears of the workers using them. Our words which help to build our House of Prayer just might be more powerful and effective if we heard ourselves speak them aloud. We can speak our words of praise out loud, declaring, "All praise and honor and glory belong to you, our wonderful God!"

Jesus is the blueprint for a House of Prayer

Jesus is the perfect example for my life of prayer. When I "walk in the same way as He walked" (1 John 2:6 ESV):

→ My steps will take me to my inner room of prayer.

→ Physically, I may be outdoors or indoors.

→ I may be alone or in a crowd.

→ The time can be any time—day or night.

→ I will enter a room decorated with rare and beautiful treasures.

→ I will enter a room where I will enjoy the pleasure of His company.

Each one of us—in mind and heart—may enter the presence of our Heavenly Father, closing out the world and all its noise and confusion. Our room can be within our mind, with lips silent—an inner place where our thoughts communicate praise along with expressing our desires to God who hears. Any time, any place we can be alone with God as we go into our room, close the door and pray to our Father who is unseen (Matthew 6:6).

Each morning our day can begin with prayer in the same way that Jesus prayed in the early morning. In the quiet at the very beginning of the day we may keep a scheduled appointment to be alone with God. It can be a time to think and clear our minds, to prepare for what the day will bring or to quiet ourselves once again from the worries and concerns of the previous day:

> "Now in the morning, having risen a long while before daylight, He went out and departed to a solitary place; and there He prayed." (Mark 1:35 ESV)

Jesus also prayed in the middle of extremely busy days that were crowded with people and their many needs. After teaching and feeding the five thousand, Jesus told his friends to go on ahead of him. He said 'good-bye' to the crowd, excused himself from His closest companions, and went off by himself to pray (Matthew 14:23).

When tension and stress increase, we need time to refresh and calm our spirit. We need to excuse ourselves and literally find a place alone. Jesus will take us to His Father, into the heavenly realm where we can enjoy the pleasure of His company even in the middle of the day!

And when the day was over, Jesus did what he often did: He knelt down and prayed (Luke 22:39-41).

Our role model gave us a blueprint for our House of Prayer. With his example written on our hearts, we, too, at the close of the day, can find delight in our Father's company. And, Jesus will be there with us. He always is! Every time we speak to God, Jesus is there at the right hand of God interceding for us (Romans 8:34). His words join with our words.

In the morning! In the middle of the day! In the evening! In the middle of the night when we cannot sleep! Jesus is always with us as we pray to our Father!

Jesus needed to pray often during the time He walked upon this earth and shared in our humanity (Hebrews 2:14). If He needed to pray often, surely we need to do the same. Jesus knows our relationship with the Father will be greatly enriched as we spend time together. The rooms in our spiritual houses will then be decorated with the beautiful treasures of joy, prayer and thanksgiving.

> "Always be joyful;
> pray continually;
> give thanks whatever happens.
> That is what God wants for you...."
>
> (1 Thessalonians 5:16-18 NCV)

Sometimes we feel shy, inept with words, ill-equipped to maintain a conversation, a little embarrassed, reluctant to begin. At times like these, when our hearts are longing for a deeper relationship with God, we join with the disciples of Jesus to request . . .

Chapter 3

"Lord, Teach Us to Pray!"
Luke 11:1

The pleasure of talking and listening to each other

> "Let us draw near to God
> With a sincere heart in full
> assurance of faith...."
> Hebrews 10:22 NIV

Leave the busy-ness of life for a while. Find a quiet place within the House of Prayer. With hearts and minds focused on Jesus, visualize Him praying often to His Father. Sensing Jesus' continual need to be in close communication with the source of His wisdom, power, and strength, let the desire of each heart be to follow His example to find wonderful delight in the pleasure of our God's company.

Every day may each one of us desire to know God more intimately. In order to develop a deeper and stronger relationship with God, time must be invested. Talking to Him. Listening to Him. Learning about each other. Sharing life's experiences. Dreaming together. Laughing. Crying. Delighting in each other's presence.

On the night He was betrayed, Jesus prayed for His disciples. He prayed also for all those who would believe in Him after He returned to His Father. In His prayer He defined the essence of eternal life. He said:

> "And this is eternal life: that they may know you, the only true God, and Jesus Christ whom you have sent" (John 17:3 ESV).

Jesus and His Father hear each person's acceptance of the invitation to come enjoy the eternal pleasure of their company when a person responds,

> "Yes, Lord, I want to know you better!"

God has promised that when we delight ourselves in Him, the desires of our hearts will be fully satisfied (Psalm 37:4). Claiming this promise, our desire to know Him will be fully satisfied! As faith deepens, diligence will bring us into the fullness of relationship that we desire.

Our Heavenly Father knows us completely, even better than good parents know their own children. God knows us so well that He even knows the number of hairs on our heads (Luke 12:6-7). He knows our names and the character of each one of us (Revelation 3:5). He knows how many tears we have shed (Psalm 56:8).

He knows so much more about us than we know about Him. But, we desire to know more about Him. We say, "I want to know you, Lord! I want to know all I can know about You, realizing that I can only know in part until I shall see You face to face and know You fully, even as I am fully known (1 Corinthians 13:12). Yes, everything I can know NOW, I want to know!"

It's true. He already knows us and knows us very well. Our Father and His Son have known us from birth, and before. They have watched us grow physically and spiritually. Like a parent who one day looks at their child and sees an adult, God and each one of us—no longer children, but rather adults—understands that the relationship must change if it is to grow deeper and reach a more mature level. In an earthly sense this is when the child—who is known so well by the parent—takes time to learn about their parent from an adult perspective. Sometimes in this world adult children never get to know their parents. They never take the time. They are not interested. Adult children desiring to know their parents better might ask: What were my parents' dreams and hopes? What happened in their lives before I was born? What difficult decisions were they forced to make? What were their joys and their disappointments? What brought them happiness . . . sadness . . . peace?

And so, we come to the Father and speak to Him in prayer. He comes to us and speaks to us through His written Word. Time spent with Him in the House of Prayer gives us an opportunity to know Him better and to understand that everything needed for life and how to follow His example and live godly comes through our knowledge of Him (2 Peter 1:3). The time spent with God in the House of Prayer is not all about what is said to Him. It's equally about what He has to say to us through His inspired word.

Time spent reading His words will give us greater insight into the mind of God. We begin to know Him better as we know more and more about Him. We begin to know Him better as we spend time talking to Him because all good relationships grow and thrive when there is daily communication.

Perhaps we are not the best of communicators, but we can learn. We can learn by example. The disciples observed Jesus praying to His Father. Undoubtedly, they already knew prayers from the prophets and psalms. Surely, they knew many traditional prayers; but it seems they realized there was something missing in the way they prayed to God. They watched Jesus as He prayed. They waited until He finished. Then one of the disciples said to him:

"Lord, teach us to pray."
Luke 11:1

Jesus' followers may have sensed in Him a stronger and more dependent connection to God. Many today, like those who witnessed Jesus praying, long for a closer connection to God through prayer. A deeper spiritual experience and a sense of real relationship are sincerely desired. Jesus taught many things, but this was one thing the apostles requested to be taught them more specifically.

The apostle Matthew heard Jesus' response to the request, "Lord, teach us to pray." And, Luke carefully listened to what he heard from witnesses who were there that day. Both Matthew and Luke recorded what Jesus said:

"This then is how you should pray,

Our Father in heaven,

Hallowed be your name.

Your kingdom come, your will be done

on earth as it is in heaven.

Give us today - each day - our daily bread.

Forgive us our sins,

as we also forgive everyone who sins against us.

And lead us not into temptation,

but deliver us from the evil one.

For yours is the kingdom

and the power

and the glory forever.

Amen."

Matthew 6:9-13 NIV and Luke 11:1-4 NIV blended

This prayer has been memorized by believers around the world. It is recited word for word in many of the world's languages. The words of this prayer, frequently called *"The Lord's Prayer,"* are often said rapidly, running sentences and words together. When the prayer is said without giving careful attention to the greater meaning, so much of the relationship with God that could be enjoyed is missed. There is a danger that praying this way could become 'babbling' (Matthew 6:7) as if there were some magic or mystical power in the very words themselves.

These beautiful words of Jesus are more than a type of prayer book repetition. They are truly a step-by-step plan for a deeper relationship with the Heavenly Father. There is a way to pray this prayer that will allow it to become more than beautiful words to be recited. It can become a path of understanding which will then lead to knowing God more intimately.

For instance, Matthew records one of the phrases Jesus expanded when He taught the prayer. He writes that first Jesus said, "When you pray, say…. 'Forgive us our sins as we also have forgiven those who sin against us" (Matthew 6:12 NIV).

Then Jesus expanded the phrase about forgiveness by adding, "For if you forgive men when they sin against you, your heavenly Father will also forgive you. But if you do not forgive men their sins, your Father will not forgive your sins" (Matthew 6:14-15 NIV).

When everything that is written in God's Word about forgiveness is combined, then the mind of God can be known and understood a little more clearly. Our closeness to Him will deepen as our knowledge of forgiveness grows. Our relationship will become more personal as we realize what forgiveness cost Him and what it will cost us.

If we develop our prayer-communication by expanding the meaning of each phrase of *'The Lord's Prayer,'* our relationship with God will improve greatly. The person who desires to enjoy the pleasure of God's company in His House of Prayer will be able to develop greater communication skills to express praise, give thanks, and make requests. Wonderful blessings await those who make the effort. Remember, desire plus diligence will bring us delight—great pleasure in His company.

Before Jesus spoke the words of prayer in response to His disciples' question, He said, "Your Father knows what you need before you ask him" (Matthew 6:8b ESV). Yes, our All-Knowing Father knows what we need; but He still wants us to ask. He desires that we speak with Him. He wants us to pray!

In quietness before opening our mouth to speak to God, we may say with the psalmist (88:9b ESV), "Every day I call upon you, O Lord; I spread out my hands to you."

Our hands have a language that expresses our inner thoughts and emotions. Fists closed in anger. Hands clapping when surprised in happiness. Hands trembling in fear. Hands constantly moving when nerves are battling worry or distress. Hands limp in sadness, disappointment, and hopelessness. Hands clenched when stress overpowers our thoughts and emotions.

Listening to the psalmist's inspired advice to spread out hands to God, it may just be best for us to actually follow the advice. And so, we physically, literally open our hands, laying them in our lap, palms up, relaxing them. In our mind we let go of everything we are holding onto. We spread out our hands!

With hands open to God, we remind ourselves that our House of Prayer begins as a House of Purity. We ask God to forgive us and to give us clean hands and a pure heart as we come into His holy presence (Psalm 24:3-4).

We confess to Him any uncleanness in our life, any sin on our hands, saying, "I wash my hands in innocence, and go around your altar, O Lord, proclaiming thanksgiving aloud, telling of all your wondrous deeds" (Psalm 26:6-7 ESV).

We thank Him for His cleansing. We tell Him how much we love being with Him, saying, "I love the house where you live, O Lord, the place where your glory dwells" (Psalm 26:8 NIV).

When we enter the presence of God with our hands open, showing our desire for a closer, more open relationship with Him, we hear how He responds to us by reading the words of the prophet Zephaniah:

> "... do not let your hands hang limp. The Lord your God is with you, he is mighty to save. He will take great delight in you, he will quiet you with his love, he will rejoice over you with sing- ing" (Zephaniah 3:17 NIV).

Our Father asks us to delight ourselves in Him because He takes great delight in us (Psalm 37:4). We find mutual delight in one another's company. Just as in our relationships with friends and loved ones here on earth, when we visit each other's homes, we come together, sit awhile and enjoy our time together. These simple pleasures of friendship may be ours when we are with God who even—listen for it—"Rejoices over us with singing" (Zephaniah 3:17 NIV).

Overcoming Enemies of Prayer

Sometimes when we plan to spend time with a special person, there can be any number of distractions. The telephone can interrupt a good conversation. Maybe something happens on the way to our visit, such as a transportation problem, an argument with someone just before we leave, a household problem, and on and on and on. By the time we reach the one we want to spend time with, we are agitated and have difficulty settling down to really enjoy our time together.

Perhaps we didn't sleep well the night before or ate too big a meal before our meeting. Our eyes droop and we have to fight to stay awake. We yawn and say, "Sorry. It's not personal." But it still interrupts the time we wanted to spend together.

And then, of course, there's the problem with our mind ... it wanders. Much as we try to listen and interact, other thoughts interrupt and we find ourselves saying, "Pardon? What did you say?" We sometimes even stop in mid-sentence and say, "Where was I going with this? I forgot what I was going to say!"

These interruptions and distractions happen with friends and family. They also happen when we try to spend time with our Heavenly Father.

Interruptions are certain to come when we desire to enter our House of Prayer to spend time with God. We must make an effort to go someplace away from the telephone, away from the doorbell, and away from the distraction of people. We must quiet every technical device, and put the cell phone on Mute. And turn off the Vibrate mode. Make an appointment with God when the fewest interruptions and distractions are anticipated. And then, keep the appointment!

Our own emotions can intrude and hinder our prayers even when we've found a quiet place to be with God. Rather than letting agitated emotions disturb conversation with the Father, take a deep breath and sit quietly until there is a calmness within. Meditate upon and follow God's inspired instructions to "Be still and know that I am God" (Psalm 46:10 ESV).

Keep your hands open, releasing everything to your Heavenly Father. Listen to soothing music if it helps. Breathe deeply and slowly. Relax.

And then, what frequently happens when we relax? Heavy eyelids ... drowsiness ... as soon as we sit and relax, we drift off. We fall asleep. It happened to Peter, James and John when Jesus, "overwhelmed with sorrow to the point of death" asked them "to stay here and keep watch with me" (Matthew 26:38 NIV). His three nearest and dearest companions were exhausted from sorrow and fell asleep instead of praying while Jesus was talking to His Father. When Jesus returned to them, rather than letting them sleep, He woke them, asking, "Why are you sleeping? Get up and pray" (Luke 22:46 ESV).

When we are exhausted because of problems and deeply serious concerns and fears, it is quite possible that Jesus would say to us, "Could you not stay awake with me for one hour? Stay awake and pray for strength against temptation" (Matthew 26:40 NCV). Sleeping, rather than praying, may be the reason we are weak in the face of what's going on in our lives.

Faint from grief. Disabled by depression. Cowardly in facing tomorrow. Paralyzed by fear. Ineffective in decision making. Anyone can become vulnerable and helpless when sleep, rather than prayer, becomes the chosen haven. Prayer in the pleasure of God's company is always the best source of strength.

After finding a quiet place to be alone, even after sitting quietly and relaxing while listening to calming music, if we feel ourselves falling asleep, stand up! Walk and talk to God! It may be a short walk from one side of the room to the other ... back and forth ... walk! With eyes open, walk and speak aloud to God! Breathe deeply. Let the sound of our own voice speaking to God help us to focus our words into a coherent, alert prayer. Let God hear our voice in prayer!

> "In the morning, O Lord, you hear my voice; in the morning I lay my requests before you and wait in expectation." (Psalm 5:3 NIV)

> "I cried out to him with my mouth; his praise was on my tongue. If I had cherished sin in my heart, the Lord would not have listened; but God has surely listened and heard my voice in prayer." (Psalm 66:17-19 NIV)

Writing down our words to God can also help to keep us focused and help to overcome those wandering thoughts that interrupt the pleasure we seek in His company.

Other hindrances to prayer that can be very destructive are the thoughts we hear in our minds—thoughts we must determine if they are truthful or filled with lies. False thoughts can sneak into our minds even when our place of prayer is quiet and we are wide awake and ready to communicate.

When we recognize a thought for the lie that it is, we need to respond from God's Word. Put God's truth into words. Here are some examples:

Lie:
God isn't interested in the day-to-day things of my life. He has bigger problems than mine. I'm not important enough to bother God with my prayers.

Truth:
"Even the sparrow finds a home, and the swallow a nest for herself, where she may lay her young, at your altars, O LORD of hosts, my King and my God." (Psalm 84:2-3 ESV)

"Look at the birds of the air: they neither sow nor reap nor gather into barns, and yet your heavenly Father feeds them. Are you not of more value than they?" (Matthew 6:26 ESV)

Response to Truth:
Even the smallest sparrow is welcome at God's altar. Therefore, since I'm told I'm more valuable than the birds of the air, I am welcome to come to Him with all my needs. **This is the truth!**

Lie:

James wrote that "the prayers of a righteous person are powerful and effective." (James 5:16 NIV)

I'm not righteous! What good are my prayers?

Truth:

"If we confess our sins, he is faithful and just and will forgive us our sins and purify us from all unrighteousness!" (1 John 1:8-9 NKJV)

My Response to Truth:

I have confessed my sins and I know He has forgiven me because He keeps His promises! He said when He forgives me He purifies me from all unrighteousness. Therefore, I am righteous in His sight and my prayers are powerful and effective. **This is the truth!**

Lie:

I cannot be bold with God. It would be arrogant and prideful.

Truth:

"In the day when I cried out, You answered me and made me bold with strength in my soul." (Psalm 138:3 NKJV)

"Let us therefore come boldly (with confidence - NIV) unto the throne of grace that we may obtain mercy, and find grace to help in time of need." (Hebrews 4:16 NKJV)

My Response to Truth:

God is the one who makes me bold. Arrogance and pride come from my own high thoughts about my own importance. But boldness comes from Him and so does the courage I need to bring my requests to Him. He has given me permission to come boldly and with confidence to receive what I need. **This is the truth!**

When lies come into our thoughts, they can be overcome by claiming God's promises. Read His promises. His words are truth. Know them well. Know what God would say in response to your thoughts. Know because you listen to Him when you read His words. Recognize lies when they come into your House of Prayer. Sweep them out just as Jesus swept through the temple. Knock them over just as Jesus knocked over the moneychangers' tables. Send them flying like the doves who escaped their cages.

And then, when the dust has settled, it's time to "go into your room, shut the door and pray to your Father" (Matthew 6:6 ESV), saying . . .

Chapter 4

"Our Father in Heaven"
Matthew 6:9

The pleasure of being in His family

> "Be still and know that I am God."
> Psalm 46:10 ESV

B e still. Relax. Don't rush. With eyes closed, see yourself coming to the Father. Feel His presence. Enjoy being with Him. He is ready to listen. Ready to respond. Trust Him.

Begin to pray as Jesus instructed. Say the words, "Our Father in heaven...." Then stop. Think about each word by itself. Let each word be a reminder of important truths and wonderful eternal blessings because of each word:

Our ... Father ... in heaven

For now, think only about the word "Our."

Jesus didn't say "My Father." He said, "Our Father." He joined Himself with the one who prays. He goes with each one of us when we go to the Father in prayer! What a delight to be surrounded by the light and truth of Jesus as we enter into the very presence of our Heavenly Father (Psalm 43:3-4).

We enjoy the pleasure of one another's company. Delightful pleasure because we are family. Jesus and each individual person. Brother and brother. Brother and sister. Family in an eternal relationship—the family relationship promised to those who would do the will of the Father in heaven (Matthew 12:50). Jesus is not ashamed to call us brothers and sisters. He brings us together into one family (Hebrews 2:11).

To be adopted as God's sons and daughters through Jesus Christ, in accordance with Our Father's pleasure and will, was His desire from before the creation of the world (Ephesians 1:3-5). He wanted the pleasure of our company. He willed it to be this way. He wanted us to be His House of Purity, holy and blameless in Our Father's sight (Ephesians 1:4) because we stand united with Jesus! Forgiven! Cleansed! Invited into His holy presence! We are the Father's children. Jesus is no longer ashamed of us. Jesus is our brother!

As we come to the Holy One who calls us "His child," meditating upon His words, we thank Him for bringing us into His family. We thank Him for our brother Jesus. We thank Him that our brother in eternity is able to bring us into His Father's presence where together we may call Him, "Our Father!"

During the years before Jesus lived as a man among men, God was recognized as *a* father . . .

- *a* father to the fatherless (Psalm 68:5)

- *a* father who has compassion on his children
  (Psalm 103:18)
- *a* father worthy of honor and respect
  (Malachi 1:6)
- *our* Father who is called Lord
  (Isaiah 63:16, 64:8)

However, God was never directly addressed as 'Father' until the Son came in the flesh to show us a more perfect way to enter the presence of God (Hebrews 9:11, 10:19). When Jesus said, "This then is how you should pray: Our Father (Matthew 6:9 NIV),"—based upon His light and truth—He began to guide His followers' thinking into a more intimate relationship, the closeness of Father and child.

From the time Jesus was twelve years old until He returned to heaven, He addressed God as 'Father.' Jesus the son was one with the Father. The Father was one with Him. Jesus did nothing by Himself. He could do only what He saw His Father doing (John 5:18-19). The relationship between God the Father and God the Son was deeply loving and intimate. They were equal. They were one.

Jesus prayed fervently regarding our relationship with His Father. In the garden just before He was arrested and taken to the cross, Jesus prayed:

> "I pray for these followers (his apostles), but I am also praying for all those who will believe in me because of their teaching. Father, I pray that they can be one. As you are in me and I am in you, I pray that they can also be one in us" (John 17:20-21 NCV).

Jesus prayed that we might enjoy this same spiritual, never-ending oneness. The Father and Son were joined in purpose and spirit. Our Father and His Son desire this same intimacy of eternal relationship with the members of their family! With us!

When Jesus takes us to the throne of God in prayer, we go as children of our Father. He tenderly and lovingly welcomes us into His affectionate embrace.

And now, let us pause and speak slowly as we add the word "Father" to the precious pronoun that includes Jesus with us. We say,

"Our Father"

We savor the joy of the love He so richly pours upon us. We rejoice in these first two words of prayer, saying:

> "How great is the love the Father has lavished
> on us, that we should be called children of God!
> And that is what we are!" (1 John 3:1 NIV)

In His prayer in the garden as He awaited His arrest and the horrendous events that would follow, Jesus was in agonizing pain, praying so earnestly that His sweat was like drops of blood falling to the ground (Luke 22:44). It was during this fervent prayer that Jesus prayed, "Abba, Father" (Mark 14:36), using the Aramaic word 'Abba' meaning 'daddy' or 'papa'—a name of relationship that, when it comes from the lips of an adult, usually expresses the deepest of heartaches and sorrows as well as feelings of helplessness.

Because we are members of God's family, God puts the Spirit of His Son in our hearts. His Spirit joins with our spirit to cry out "Abba, Father" (Galatians 4:6). During our times of anguish and grief, "the Spirit helps us in our weakness. We do not know what to pray for as we ought, but the Spirit himself intercedes for us with groanings too deep for words" (Romans 8:26 ESV). It is by the Spirit that we may pray, "Abba, Father" (Romans 8:15).

Because of Jesus we share in this wonderful Father and child relationship. We may address Our Father by the most intimate of names with childlike trust as we call Him "Abba." And, as we add the word "Father" to the word 'Abba'—the name expressing the dependency of a child upon the Father—we join the most intimate name with our intellectual understanding and sincere appreciation for being invited to call Him "Our Father."

We are very precious to God. We are His children. Our relationship deepens as we reflect upon some of the many wonderful blessings that come with the privilege of calling Him, "Abba, Father."

We have:

- the same life that He has ... eternal!
    (John 3:36)
- the same home that He has ... eternal!
    (Romans 8:17)
- a new character, like His
    (2 Corinthians 5:17)
- security and love that nothing can take away
    (John 10:28-29)
- all the basic necessities for our daily lives
    (Matthew 6:30)

51

- all the necessities for our spiritual lives
  (2 Peter 1:3)
- promises and more promises to help us
  (2 Peter 1:4)

The Wonderful Privilege to have Jesus for a Brother

Jesus prayed, "Abba, Father... all things are possible for you" (Mark 14:36 ESV).

We may pray, "...Abba, Father. The Spirit himself bears witness with our spirit that we are children of God" (Romans 8:15-17 ESV).

Abba
Aramaic, spoken by infants and children expressing complete love and trust

Father
Expresses an intellectual understanding of the father-child relationship

Abba, Father
Expresses love and complete trust along with intellectual understanding

---

When Jesus prayed, "Abba, Father," He immediately said, "Everything is possible for you (Mark 14:36 NIV)!"

Calling God by the most intimate of names should always remind us that with our Abba, Father, nothing is impossible. Our Father knows the things on our hearts and in our minds that we think are absolutely impossible. He wants us to trust Him with the impossible.

In our opening words of prayer, we may always say with confidence, "Abba, Father, everything is possible for you!"

With God all things are possible! All things!

Before moving any further in our prayer, we may pause, giving our problems and concerns into the loving care of Our Father. We will remember that we have been encouraged to "not be anxious about anything, but in everything, by prayer and petition, with thanksgiving to present our requests to God. And the peace of God, which transcends all understanding, will guard our hearts and minds in Christ Jesus" (Philippians 4:6-7 NIV). And so, when problems and concerns seem impossible to solve, we tell Our Father about them; and then, wait quietly for His peace to calm us.

Almost all of us have a loved one—from among those nearest and dearest to us—who is walking through life in a direction away from Our Father. Perhaps we have done everything we know to do, said everything we can possibly say, and still our heart is heavy knowing that if Jesus were to come today, the person who is so precious to us would not be welcomed into heaven.

We may have given up hope or settled into quiet despair, asking God the same question that was asked of Jesus so long ago, "Who then can be saved (Matthew 19:25 ESV)?"

This is just one example of what might seem impossible. When it seems impossible for us, Jesus' words are there to encourage us, "With God all things are possible!"

Pondering this thought, we may say to Our Father, "If you can do anything for my loved one, please work in their life to bring them to you." Jesus, who is the same yesterday, today, and forever (Hebrews 13:8), would reply to us as He replied so long ago, "If you can? All things are possible for the one who believes" (Mark 9:22-23 ESV).

May we be like the man who answered Jesus and may we also exclaim, "I do believe; help me overcome my unbelief" (Mark 9:24 NIV). May we, in prayer to Our Father, ask Him to help us overcome our unbelief so that we might have renewed hope in the power of prayer, renewed joy in the pleasure of His company, and renewed trust that with Him all things are possible!

Those with their hearts turned away from Our Father are not only those in our own families. They are everywhere—from the house next door to the most distant place on the opposite side of the world. Think about them! Pray for them! Ask God to do the impossible! Tell Him we believe He is able to do whatever can be done to change the hardened hearts of those who are outside His family.

Having moved slowly and thoughtfully through the first two words of the prayer Jesus taught, we are ready to add two more words, saying,

"Our Father in Heaven"

We close our eyes in order to see the heavenly realm more clearly. "We fix our eyes not on what is seen, but on what is unseen. For what is seen is temporary, but what is unseen is eternal" (2 Corinthians 4:18 NIV).

While visualizing the heavenly realm during our time of prayer, we must not be too quick to speak. We give our mind and heart time to grasp the reality of the unseen. We visualize Jesus, our brother standing by our side "dressed in a robe reaching down to his feet and with a golden sash around his chest. His head and hair white like wool, as white as snow, and his eyes like blazing fire. His feet like bronze glowing in a furnace, and his voice like the sound of rushing waters. His face like the sun shining in all its brilliance" (Revelation 1:12-16 NIV).

We see Jesus standing ready to guide us to the altar of God Our Father—to God, our joy and our delight (Psalm 43:3-4). We place our right hand into the hand of Jesus, our brother and guide.

With the same words of the psalmist we may say:

> "I am always with you; you hold me by my right hand. You guide me with your counsel, and afterward you will take me into glory. Whom have I in heaven but you? And earth has nothing I desire besides you" (Psalm 73:23-25 NIV).

Then, as Jesus instructed His disciples who requested, "Teach us to pray," we pray to Our Father who is unseen (Matthew 6:6) believing that Our Father who sees what is done in secret will reward us (Matthew 6:18). He will give us the desires of our hearts as He has promised.

Seeing into the heavenly realm, hand in hand with Jesus, we begin to sense and truly believe how welcome we are in Our Father's presence. By faith in the reality of what we cannot now see with our physical eyes, we rejoice because every time we pray we join the company of innumerable—thousands upon thousands—joyful angels. We will be praying in the company of our Father and His Son Jesus our mediator (Hebrews 12:22-24a).

Our Father waits for us to speak and to continue in prayer. We lean toward Jesus, who reminds us, "When you pray, say . . .

Chapter 5

"Hallowed be Your Name"
Luke 11: 2

The pleasure of learning more about Him

> "Glory in his holy name;
> let the hearts of those who
> seek the LORD rejoice!"
> Psalm 105:3 ESV

Holy, Holy, Holy sing the angels around the throne of Our Father in Heaven! As we draw near to Him, hand in hand with Jesus our mediator, the clarity of our vision into the eternal realm of God begins to improve. Through the eyes of the prophet Isaiah (6:1-7), we see Our Father seated upon a throne, high and exalted. Angels called seraphim fly around Him. They are calling to one another:

> "Holy, holy, holy is the Lord Almighty;
> the whole earth is full of his glory."
> Isaiah 6:3 NIV

As we approach the awesome presence of God in prayer, we hold the hand of Jesus even tighter. Our first thoughts could very well be like those of Isaiah, "I am ruined! Because I

(have) unclean lips, and I live among a people of unclean lips"
(Isaiah 6:5 NASB).

However, looking from Almighty God to Jesus, we do not find
condemnation. We find courage and acceptance in the presence
of Our Holy Father. We do not need to fear because we live in
His love and His spirit lives in us. We are in Him and He is in
us! In Jesus all fear is gone (1 John 4:13-18)!

Seeing with eyes of faith—seeing and standing in prayer at the
very throne of God, our vision sharpens through the revelation
of Jesus given to the apostle John. Like Isaiah, he also saw the
seraphim around the throne of God. John told us that day and
night they never stop saying,

> "Holy, holy, holy
> is the Lord God Almighty,
> who was, and is, and is to come."
> Revelation 4:8 ESV

The words of the seraphim confirm for us–as we approach God
to speak–that Our Father is Eternal God. He deserves all the
glory and honor, all the thanksgiving and praise that our hearts
and minds can form into words. Before we speak in prayer,
we pause a moment longer to see those in heaven who are
worshiping before the throne. We join them in praise, saying,

> "You are worthy, our Lord and God,
> to receive glory and honor and power,"
> Revelation 4:11 NIV

Once again, because of God's written word, we hear Jesus saying, "This then is how you should pray" so that from our lips come His words,

"Hallowed be your name!"

From Genesis 1:1 through Revelation 22:21 God reveals more and more about Himself so that each of us who seek to know Him better may deepen our relationship with Him. More than one hundred different names for the Father, Son and Holy Spirit open the way for each of us to know Him more intimately. Just as no one really knows who we ourselves are until they know and understand fully the names by which we are called—first name, middle name, family name, father, mother, son, daughter, friend, co-worker, confidant—no one will ever really know God until His names are understood.

In today's world we hear God's name and the name of His Son Jesus Christ spoken frequently. Misused and abused. From lips of unbelievers, and sometimes even from believers as well, come expletives, vulgar language, and joking that dishonor the Lord of glory. God has said that He "will not hold anyone guiltless who misuses His name" (Exodus 20:7 NIV).

As each one prays the words "Hallowed be your name," boldly and with conviction, we need also to say, "When I speak your name, God, I will speak it only with love, honor and respect!"

In adoration we tell God, that His name is holy to us. We tell Him that we will honor His name by setting it apart from all common language. We tell Him that we will use His name only in an atmosphere of glory and humble respect.

We can praise the name of Our Father by reading aloud the
words the Spirit of God inspired Daniel to write so long ago:

> "Blessed be the name of God forever and ever,
> to whom belong wisdom and might.
> He changes times and seasons;
> He removes kings and sets up kings;
> He gives wisdom to the wise
> and knowledge to those who have understanding;
> He reveals deep and hidden things;
> He knows what is in the darkness,
> and the light dwells with Him."
>
> Daniel 2:20-23 ESV

As we think about these beautiful words of praise—words that
compliment God for who He is and what He has done—we have
an opportunity to express our faith by making these words even
more personal. We rephrase Daniel's words to express directly
to Our Father who He is to us:

> *Blessed be __YOUR__ name, God, forever and ever;*
> *wisdom and power are __YOURS__.*
> *__YOU__ change times and seasons.*
> *__YOU__ remove kings and set them up.*
> *__YOU__ give wisdom to the wise and knowledge*
> *to those who have understanding.*
> *__YOU__ reveal deep and hidden things;*
> *__YOU__ know what is in darkness, and*
> *the light of __JESUS__ dwells with __YOU__!*

Names of God

An exercise in meditation:

Read through all the names of God on the list that follows.

For daily praise, choose one name that meets your need of the moment.

Call God by that name and tell Him why this name means something personal to you at this particular time.

Say boldly:
I PRAISE YOU BECAUSE YOUR NAME IS

- ☐ Almighty God (Genesis 17:1; Isaiah 54:5; Jeremiah 31:35; 2 Corinthians 6:17,18; Revelation 1:8)
- ☐ Advocate (Job 16:19-21; 1 Timothy 2:5; Hebrews 7:25 and 9:24)
- ☐ Bread of life (Exodus 25:30; Deuteronomy 8:3; Psalm 23:5; John 6:35)
- ☐ Creator (Genesis 1:1, 26; Colossians 1:15-16)
- ☐ Emmanuel (Isaiah 7:14; Matthew 1:22-23)
- ☐ Eternal God (Genesis 21:33; Exodus 15:18; 1 John 5:20)
- ☐ Everlasting Father (Isaiah 9:6; John 3:16; John 6:44-47)
- ☐ Friend (Isaiah 41:8; John 15:14-15)
- ☐ God of Comfort (Jeremiah 8:18; Romans 15:5; 2 Corinthians 1:3-7)
- ☐ God of the House of God (Genesis 35:7; Ephesians 1:22-23; Colossians 1:18)
- ☐ God of My Life (Psalm 42:8; Acts 17:28)
- ☐ Guardian of my Soul (Job 10:12,14; Romans 8:31-39;1 Peter 2:25)
- ☐ Helper (Psalm 118:7; Hebrews 13:6)
- ☐ High Priest (Hebrews 2:17; 3:1; 4:14-15)
- ☐ Hope (Psalm 71:5; Matthew 12:21; Romans 15:13)
- ☐ Husband (Isaiah 54:5; Revelation 21:2,9)
- ☐ IAM THAT IAM (Genesis 2:4; Exodus 3:14; John 8:58-59; Hebrews 13:8; Revelation 1:8)
- ☐ IAM Healer (Exodus 15:26; Psalm 23:3; Psalm 147:3; 1 Peter 2:24)
- ☐ IAM Judge (Judges 11:27; John 8:50)

☐ IAM Life and Truth (Psalm 31:1; John 16:13)

☐ IAM Light (Psalm 27:1; John 8:12)

☐ IAM the LORD Who is All Powerful (Psalm 147:5)

☐ IAM the LORD Who is Always There (Matthew 28:20; 2 Corinthians 6:16, Romans 8:39)

☐ IAM the LORD Who Makes You Holy (Exodus 31:13; Leviticus 20:7,8; Psalm 23:5; John 17:17; 1 Corinthians 1:2; Jude 24)

☐ IAM the LORD Who Sees You (Genesis 16:13; Psalm 33:13-14; John 4:29 and 6:64; Hebrews 4:13)

☐ IAM Peace (Judges 6:24; Isaiah 9:6; Psalm 23:2, John 14:27; Romans 5:1; Philippians 4:6-7; Colossians 3:15; 2 Thessalonians 3:16)

☐ IAM Provider (Genesis 22:14; Matthew 6:31-33; Philippians 4:19)

☐ IAM Your Refuge (Jeremiah 16:9-21; Psalm 91:9; John 17:11)

☐ IAM Righteousness (Jeremiah 23:5,6; 1 Corinthians 1:30)

☐ IAM the Rock (Genesis 49:24; Psalm 18:2; 1 Corinthians 10:4)

☐ IAM Shepherd (Psalm 23:1, Isaiah 40:11,John 10:14ff; 1 Peter 2:25)

☐ IAM Your Victory Banner (Exodus 17:15; Psalm 23:4; 1 Corinthians 15:57;2 Corinthians 2:14; 1 John 5:4-5)

☐ King Most High (Psalm 47:2; John 1:49 and 18:33-37; 1 Timothy 6:15)

☐ Lamb of God (John 1:29; Revelation 13:8)

☐ Love (Psalm 59:17; 1 John 4:8,16)

☐ Savior (Psalm 88:1; Matthew 1:21, Luke 2:11; John 2:42)

As each one reads through the alphabetical list of the *Names of God*, because of present circumstances—whether joyful or problematic—one or more of the names will touch your heart.

It may be that you praise God whose name is 'Bread of Life' because even now He is strengthening and nourishing you in your prayer life. He satisfies your spiritual hunger with delight and wonderful pleasure as you are drawn closer to Him.

In a time of loneliness, the intimate name you call God could be 'Friend.' In a time of thanksgiving, the name that endears Him even more to you might be 'I AM Provider!' When you have been hurt by someone you love and trust, 'I AM Healer' when spoken with understanding can allow His healing in you to begin.

Each time you praise God for who He is in your own personal life, you are thanking Him for His unfailing love, for His faithfulness and loyalty, and for His truthful words. You are expressing to Him that His words of promise are confirmed by all the honor of His name (Psalm 138:2).

Our Heavenly Father is honorable and trustworthy. "For no matter how many promises God has made, they are 'Yes' in Christ" (2 Corinthians 1:20 NIV). God always honors His word. He keeps every promise He has made. When we praise Him for who He is, we give Him the highest honor.

There are times when our prayer life may feel like we are members of the church in Laodicea. Instead of Jesus speaking about our deeds, He might say of our prayers, or lack of them, "I hear your words of prayer; they are neither cold nor hot. I wish your prayers were either one or the other" (Revelation 3:15).

If our prayer life is 'hot'—sincere, disciplined, consistent, fervent—our enthusiasm and joy in speaking with Our Father will be bringing Him pleasure and delight. If our prayer life has grown 'cold', Jesus will come knocking to encourage us once again, saying,

> "Here I am! I stand at the door and knock. If you hear my voice and open the door, I will come in and eat with you and you with me" (Revelation 3:20 NCV).

As we feed on and live by every word that comes from the mouth of God (Matthew 4:4), we eat with Him and He with us just as He has promised. Jesus comes knocking on our spiritual door, inviting us to accept His invitation to overcome a lethargic prayer life by sitting with Him and Our Father more frequently and enthusiastically.

Meditating, still seeing the unseen, we rejoice in our privileged seating assignment. "Because of his great love for us, God, who is rich in mercy, made us alive with Christ even when we were dead in transgressions.... And God raised us up with Christ and seated us with him in the heavenly realms in Christ Jesus" (Ephesians 2:4-6 NIV).

Seeing the eternal reality of being seated in such a place of love and protection, enjoying the pleasure of being in the company of the Father and Son, we turn to Our Father and join with Jesus to rejoice and say boldly, "I praise you, Father, Lord of heaven and earth" (Luke 10:21).

Then we turn to Jesus to acknowledge that we truly believe He is who He said He is, reconfirming our faith that His name is

'Son.' We confess again and again that God the Father has sent His Son to be the Savior of the world. We reaffirm that Jesus is the Son of God and that the Father lives in Him and He is in God (1 John 4:14-15).

We confess that Jesus Christ is Lord, to the glory of God the Father. We thank Our Father for exalting Jesus to the highest place and giving Him the name that is greater than any other name, so that everyone should bow to their knees—everyone in heaven and on earth and under the earth (Philippians 2:9-11). We confess boldly in prayer, "Jesus Christ, you are the Son of God and you are my Lord!"

Knowing that our mouths will speak the things that are in our hearts (Matthew 12:34), saying the names of God in prayer and praise will truly express the depths of our faith and love. Every time we express our love for Him, a wonderful enthusiasm will fill us as we tell Him what He means to us.

Now, linger awhile longer in the courts of heaven before moving further into prayer. Look around. Let your focus in the spiritual realm become clearer. See the Holy Spirit everywhere . . . encircling the throne and filling heaven . . . hovering over His House of Prayer . . . filling us with joy and peace as we trust in Him so that we overflow with hope (Romans 15:13).

The Spirit of truth, whom Jesus promised would be with us forever (John 14:16), is the same Spirit who surrounds us as we sit on the throne between Father and Son. The Spirit's name not only promises us truth, His name promises us wisdom from above and brings real understanding. We are invited to share in the Spirit's wise counsel and abundant power. He brings true knowledge as well as awesome fear and respect for Our Father. The result is delight—the delight that is found at the throne of God (Isaiah 11:2-3, Psalm 43:4)!

The apostle Paul prayed a blessing upon the early Christians. It is a blessing inspired by the Spirit of truth. The blessing has been preserved, and is intended for every Christian to claim as their own:

> "The grace of the Lord Jesus Christ,
> and the love of God,
> and the fellowship of the Holy Spirit
> be with you all."
> 2 Corinthians 13:14 ESV

The relationship with God that we long to become stronger and deeper is growing as we pray through the first two phrases of the words Jesus taught, "Our Father in heaven, hallowed be your name." We are learning to know Him better and to understand the most loving and intimate names that we may call Him. Names filled with promise and blessing. Names filled with undying love.

It is with wonderful joy that by faith we receive the blessing given and respond to God,

> *"The grace of <u>MY</u> Lord Jesus Christ*
> *and the love of <u>MY</u> Heavenly Father*
> *and the fellowship of the Holy Spirit*
> *is <u>WITH ME!</u>"*
> 2 Corinthians 13:14 ESV personalized

Our Father who hears when we speak our words of prayer and affirmation finds His delight in our love and praise. And, even though we might desire to continue praising and thanking God by confessing His wonderful names of promise and salvation, He is ready for us to continue our prayer.

And so, we pray . . .

Chapter 6

"Your Kingdom Come"

Matthew 6:10a

The pleasure of unity with the King

> "Lift up your heads, O
> gates! … lift them up …
> that the King of glory
> may come in.
> Who is this King of glory?
> The Lord of hosts, he is
> the King of glory!"
> Psalm 24:9-10 ESV

Daily open your heart so that the "King of glory may come in." Raise the gates of your mind. Draw closer to God. Rejoice in the pleasure of His company. Delight yourself in Him. Lift up your thoughts and open yourself to an ever-deepening relationship with your Lord and King. Ask Him to take His rightful place. Ask Him to be seated in the place of highest importance—upon the throne within you.

In prayerful meditation each one should ask, "Have I truly given God the highest place in my mind, in my heart and in my soul? Does the King of Glory, the Lord Almighty, really sit on the throne of my heart? Am I allowing Him to rule my life? Do I daily seek the King's wise counsel? Are my decisions guided by the King's wisdom?"

As we test ourselves with these questions, our affirmation of desire will be spoken in the next phrase that Jesus taught,

"Your Kingdom come!"

Now, pausing to think more about Jesus who is our Eternal King (1 Timothy 1:17) and visualizing His throne, reflect upon the truth expressed in our King's words, "God's kingdom is coming, but not in a way that you will be able to see with your eyes. People will not say, 'Look, here it is!' or, 'There it is!' because God's kingdom is within you" (Luke 17:20-21 NCV). Let us rejoice because His kingdom within us will never end (Luke 1:33)!

Each day we must test who or what receives the greatest portion of our time and attention. We examine ourselves. We test ourselves (2 Corinthians 13:5). We look at our life to be certain that Jesus is reigning as King over everything we think, speak and do. We ask ourselves "Am I seeking His righteousness and His kingdom first" (Matthew 6:33).

Daily concerns, problems, family responsibilities, work—so many things can crowd out the time we spend honoring our King and delighting in the pleasures of His company. Even though we may have previously crowned Jesus as our King, sometimes circumstances, relationships, our worries and fears, and even our own racing thoughts shout for our attention, crowding our King into an ever-shrinking amount of time and space in our lives. Time with our King can become so minimized that we are no longer able to squeeze meaningful prayers into our tight schedules. Jesus receives less and less attention because of our 'busy-ness.' The things that we 'must' do each day and throughout the week can cram waking hours so tightly that they choke out the time we might be enjoying in the pleasure of our King's company.

The kingdom of God that is a matter of righteousness, peace and joy in the Holy Spirit (Romans 14:17) offers us so many blessings if we will just re-evaluate and restructure our priorities. If there is worry and anxiety instead of the peace that passes understanding (Philippians 4:4-7), and if the joy of prayer has dissolved into apathy and procrastination, what we see upon examining ourselves may show that the kingdom of God within us is no longer of first importance. It may mean that we are not opening the gates of our hearts and minds to welcome our King in purposeful praise and prayer.

If our personal examination proves this to be true, then once again we must say to Our Father, "I will be a House of Purity!" It is time to spiritually clean and re-organize priorities within our House of Prayer. We carefully set aside those things in our lives that are crowding out our time of prayer with the King. Our worries and concerns must once again be placed into His hands for His consideration and working. We give God, and God alone, the place of supreme importance. We do not let anything crowd out our time with Him.

Daily we may come boldly to bow before our King Jesus who is seated upon His throne in the kingdom that is within us. We praise our King, calling Him by some of His many descriptive names:

"Faithful and True! Word of God! King of kings! Lord of lords!"
Revelation 19:11-16

Wonderful names! We praise Jesus as our King! We thank Him because He is the Word, Our Father's communication to us. He has communicated to us everything we need to know in order to live and serve Him in His kingdom (2 Peter 1:3). We praise Him because everything that has been written in Scripture bears His holy and hallowed name, Faithful and True!

The joyful peace which is the very atmosphere of the kingdom of God will return to us when we praise Jesus because He is our personal King, sitting on the throne of our own heart. The joy that is ever-present in the kingdom of God will return as we rejoice in the Lord always. We claim God's promise that if we will not be anxious about anything, but pray with thanksgiving and make our requests known to Him, His peace which is beyond our understanding will guard our hearts and minds in Christ Jesus (Philippians 4:4-7).

Can you remember the day you knew you loved Jesus and knew with certainty that you wanted to spend eternity with Him? Do you remember the commitment you made to love, obey and serve Him all the days of your life and beyond? Remember that moment in time!

Think of the very moment when you entered the kingdom of God and when your loving Savior added you to His eternal family (Acts 2:47).

You heard Jesus' words declare, "Truly, truly, I say to you, unless one is born again he cannot see the kingdom of God. Truly, truly, I say to you, unless one is born of water and the Spirit, he cannot enter the kingdom of God" (John 3:3, 5 ESV).

When were you born again? When were you born of water and the spirit? When did you become a citizen of heaven (Ephesians 2:19, Philippians 3:20)? When did you leave the kingdom of this world and enter the kingdom of God?

Even though we understand very clearly from Jesus that God's kingdom is within a person and it's coming cannot be seen with physical eyes (Luke 17:20-21), we can give a specific date to our new birth. We may go back to the exact time and event with confidence knowing that Jesus brought us into His kingdom on that day because we heard His call of love and with full trust and faith obeyed His command to be born of water and Spirit. We were buried with Him and by His Spirit we were raised from the water just as the Spirit of God raised Jesus from the dead. We entered His kingdom a new person! Born again! Born of water and the Spirit!

When we entered the kingdom of God and His kingdom entered us, it was an answer to Jesus' prayer in the Garden of Gethsemane. Jesus prayed that in the same way the Father and Son are united in spirit that all of us who would believe in Him through the apostles' message "may all be one just as you, Father, are in me and I in you" (John 17:21 ESV).

Our Father's love and Jesus in us! What joy is ours! What joy there is in heaven! Wonderful joy expressed in the presence of the angels of God over each sinner who repents and changes their heart and life (Luke 15:10). Our Father and His Son, our King, rejoiced over us! And they continue to rejoice as each one of us comes in prayer to "the living God... to thousands upon thousands of angels in joyful assembly" (Hebrews 12:22 NIV).

We come to the throne of God in prayer, and with spiritual ears we hear, "Hallelujah! For the Lord our God, the Almighty, reigns... for the marriage of the Lamb has come and His bride has made herself ready. Blessed are those who are invited to the marriage supper of the Lamb" (Revelation 19:6-7, 9 NASB).

These are the true words of God (Revelation 19:9). These are His true words about the wedding, His bride, and the wedding supper of the Lamb who is Jesus (John 1:36). We have been invited into the presence and pleasure of the company of our King—our King, who as a bridegroom rejoices over His bride (Isaiah 62:5). Jesus rejoices over each one who enters into His kingdom and joins together with all the saved who share the relationship of bride to bridegroom.

Speaking about Jesus, John the Baptist said that he himself was the friend of the bridegroom and that he rejoiced greatly at the bridegroom's voice. He said, "This joy is mine" (John 3:29 NIV). This joy is ours also! This joy is ours as we continually hear God calling and inviting us into fellowship with Himself and with His Son, Jesus Christ (1 John 1:3).

God's Word tells us that when a man is united to his wife, the two become one flesh (Matthew 19:5). It's called 'a marriage.' When we made our eternal commitment to our King, promising to love and cherish Him for eternity, we became one with him in spirit (1 Corinthians 6:17).

We who are members of His body, called His church (Ephesians 5:28-30), are promised to one husband, to Christ (2 Corinthians 11:2 NIV). Christ loves His church, His bride. He gave everything for His bride. Christ continues to make His bride holy and pure, cleansing her by the washing with water through His words. Yes, His church—His bride—is fed, dressed, and cared for so that she has every opportunity to grow into a deeper relationship with Him. He is preparing His bride to be presented into eternity—glorious, splendid and radiant, without stain or wrinkle or any other blemish, but holy and blameless (Ephesians 5:25-32).

His bride—His body, His church—rejoices and gives Him glory, as she makes herself ready. Christ's bride dresses in the fine linen—bright and clean—of righteous acts and loving deeds of service (Revelation 19:7-8).

Our Father joins in dressing us appropriately for eternity. Our soul rejoices in our God who clothes us with garments of salvation and arrays us in robes of righteousness (Isaiah 61:10).

We are dressed as the bride of Jesus, our King. We are dressed in salvation—in clothes that make us presentable to Our Father. "For all of us who were baptized into Christ have clothed ourselves with Christ" (Galatians 3:27 NASB). We have been clothed spiritually with Christ Himself. We are clothed in absolute sinlessness and purity!

Being 'one spirit' with Jesus and clothed in the purest of clothing, we daily renew our pledge of faithfulness. As we stand at the throne of God, with Jesus holding us by our right hand, we may respond with our personal vow to the familiar questions asked of so many brides in Christian weddings around the world. If the name of Jesus were to be spoken where the groom's name is mentioned, the vows requiring our response might sound like this:

> "Will you have the bridegroom Jesus Christ
> to be your wedded husband,
> to live together according to God's plan,
> in holy marriage?
> Will you serve Him, love, honor, and keep Him
> in sickness and in health;
> and forsaking all others
> keep yourself only for Him,
> so long as you both shall live?"

May each one who now bears the name 'bride' respond, "I will."

The bride of the King will vow—not once but daily at His throne—to be faithful to Him for as long as they both shall live. Now and for all eternity!

Having said our vows in the hearing of the Father and in the presence of angels in the heavenly realm, our relationship of continually renewed commitment will daily bring us love, joy, peace, patience, kindness, goodness, faithfulness, and self-control (Galatians 5:22) as we live by the Spirit and keep in step with the Spirit of Jesus Christ (Galatians 5:25).

In traditional Christian weddings, following the vows, the minister will turn to those witnesses who are present to hear the promises made by the bridegroom and bride, saying,

"Therefore, what God has joined together, let man not separate" (Matthew 19:6 NKJV).

Our Heavenly Father desires that nothing will separate His Son and those who are united to Him. He wants Jesus and His bride to be together eternally. Even though He knows there will be many pressures and strains upon the relationship, Our Father has the power to keep the believer and the bridegroom together forever.

We, the bride of Christ, may encourage ourselves with these God-breathed words, reading slowly and savoring each word:

> "Who shall separate us from the love of Christ?
> Shall trouble or hardship or persecution
> or famine or nakedness
> or danger or sword?
> No, in all these things
> we are more than conquerors
> through him who loved us.
> For I am convinced
> that neither death nor life,
> neither angels nor demons,
> neither the present nor the future,
> nor any powers,
> neither height nor depth,
> nor anything else in all creation,
> will be able to separate us
> from the love of God
> that is in Christ Jesus our Lord."
> Romans 8:35, 37-39 NIV

With vows renewed, our commitment and promises reaffirmed, and continuing in an attitude of prayer and meditation, it is time to make the House of Prayer a home—a home where children of God will be added and the family will grow.

Always hand in hand, the bridegroom and we His bride turn to face whatever may come in life. We live and walk together. We share each day. We talk about everything. We listen to one another. We keep no secrets. We love, honor and cherish each other as we continue to build on earth as it is in heaven.

What will the future hold? What will happen next? How will our relationship grow into even greater delight? Diligent to do Our Father's will in all things, our prayer continues . . .

Chapter 7

"Your Will Be Done
On Earth as it is in Heaven"

Matthew 6:10b

The pleasure of wanting what He wants

"The Spirit and the bride say, 'Come!'
And let the one who hears say, 'Come!'"

Revelation 22:17 ESV

L iving in marriage! Jesus our beloved husband and
we—His pure and chaste bride—are united and
grow more deeply in our loving relationship. We find
delight and constant joy in the pleasure of one another's
company.

As we live our lives in this precious and intimate relationship,
we—the bride of Christ—are being transformed into His
likeness with ever-increasing glory which comes from the Spirit.
Our faces are turned to Jesus, our husband and bridegroom
(2 Corinthians 3:16, 18). It's as if the bridal veil has been lifted
so we may see Him more clearly in order to become more
like Him.

Our 'one spirit' relationship with Jesus changes us as Our Father has promised. Nothing comes between Him and us. We openly reflect the likeness of Jesus—our brother, friend, King and husband. His light shines upon us, brightening our faces with joy, illuminating our minds with understanding, and burning ever brighter within our hearts. Our Father hears our prayers and the light from His face shines upon our unveiled faces (Psalm 4:6-8).

Rejoicing in the love of our Eternal Husband we think about the many desires we want Him to consider. However, before expressing our desires and asking Him to give to us, we think about what He wants. Our own needs and desires will be met, but are we prayerfully considering His desires! What does He want? What is His perfect will for His bride, His church? What does He want for all of His people? What does He want in the heavenly realm? Knowing what He desires in heaven helps us to know His will here on earth. And so, we pause in prayer and observe with eyes of faith!

Jesus who has become for us all wisdom from God has opened the way through His teaching on prayer for us to express to Our Father how much we want to bring joy to Him. We long for our relationship on earth to be as much as possible like it is, and will be in heaven. We know that for now we see and know things only partially. There is so much more that we will know later when we shall see Him face to face (1 Corinthians 13:12). But, for now, before leaving this earth to live fully in eternity, we want to experience the best of His love. We want to reflect Him more perfectly as His will is understood and given the highest priority in our lives.

And so, repeating the words Jesus taught, we say,

"Your will be done
on earth as it is in heaven!"

Having been born again, the assurance that we can *'see'* the kingdom of God is ours (John 3:3). By faith in God's Word, there is enough said about heavenly activity for us to do here on earth what is being done in the unseen heavenly realm.

David the psalmist was privileged to receive inspiration from the Spirit of God so he could reveal for us what the angels are doing in heaven. Listen and see with eyes of faith:

> "The Lord has established his throne in heaven,
> and His kingdom rules over all.
> Praise the Lord, you his angels,
> you mighty ones who do His bidding,
> who obey His Word.
> Praise the Lord, all his heavenly hosts,
> you his servants who do his will."
>
> Psalm 103:19-21 NIV underlining for emphasis by author

In speaking these words in prayer, "Your will be done on earth as it is in heaven," both a request and a proclamation are made. We are asking Our Father to do all He can in our present world to bring about His will in the hearts and lives of all people, as well as in the decisions of leaders and rulers of the countries of the world (1 Timothy 2:1-2). We are also proclaiming that we agree with whatever His will might be.

After praying for His will to be done, we pause to reflect upon the heavenly realm as David described it. We read that His kingdom rules over all. When we voiced the words "Your kingdom come," we expressed to God our desire for Him to rule in our lives as well as in the lives of our family and our friends, our community, our country and throughout the world.

Then we read that His angels are instructed to praise the Lord. Along with the angels, we praise Him here on earth, knowing that our praises reach Him in heaven. We praise Him when we lift up His name, when we respect and honor His name, and when we call Him by those names that reveal His desire to meet our needs. In doing so, we express our gratitude to Him.

The Lord tells us that in heaven His angels come when they are called. They hear the Father's requests and follow His instructions. They obey His words. Those in the heavenly kingdom are servants who do His will.

Understanding what is done by angels in heaven gives us words of prayer to form requests for ourselves on earth. The desire of our heart is to become more and more a servant doing His will, listening to His instructions found in His words, and obeying whatever He has commanded.

All his angels worship Him (Hebrews 1:6). They come to Him in joyful assembly (Hebrews 12:22). We pray that our delight will be to worship Him always. If our attitudes about joining with the family of God have become lukewarm or are no longer of first importance, at this time in our prayer a heartfelt sorrow will lead us to repent, making a new commitment to assemble regularly with our family of believers. God can and will renew our joy in the fellowship of His church on earth just as it is in heaven.

The plan of salvation that was in the mind of God even before the creation of the world found its complete fulfillment in Jesus—in His death, burial, and resurrection. Although Jesus came from heaven and returned to heaven, the fulfillment of all that God planned took place on earth. These things are celebrated here on earth as well as in heaven. Heaven and earth are joined together in Jesus for as long as time shall last. If in heaven even angels have a longing and desire to look into these things (1 Peter 1:12), shouldn't we open our Bibles and rejoice in our reading and study. The will of God is done on earth as in heaven when His written word is read and reread.

Jesus is now in the heavenly realm at the right hand of God where all angels, authorities, and powers are subject to him (1 Peter 3:21-22). When we go to the throne of God, we stand hand in hand with Jesus (Psalm 73:23). We stand with the angels. Together with the heavenly beings we live our lives in submission to Him.

As we confirm to God our personal desire to do on earth what is done in heaven, our time in meditative prayer is perfect for renewing our vows to place our will into a 'one spirit' relationship with His will. It becomes a time for the renewal of vows between the bride and bridegroom. We say to God:

"I again commit my life to you, O God of Love,
      promising to follow you—faithful to the end.
May my mind be captured by your sufficiency;
      May my heart be filled with your love;
      May my hands be lifted to your praise;
      May my knees be bowed to your majesty;

> May my life be transformed into your likeness;
> May my vows be faithfully kept forever!"
> (By permission from Mike Cope, "One Holy Hunger")

We ask God to help us do in our lives what is being done in heaven. We ask Him to teach us to do His will because He is Our Father (Psalm 143:10)!

We ask Him to help us live in accordance with the Spirit and to have our minds set on what the Spirit desires (Romans 8:5). We look for His will in all things, knowing that He has promised we will find His will if we truly seek it.

At times when it is difficult to obey Our Father's will, we look to Jesus, our heavenly role model. We remember in the garden when Jesus prayed, telling the Father that what He must do was very difficult and if there was any way He could be released from what faced him, an alternate plan would be welcomed. Even before the thought was finished, Jesus prayed, "Nevertheless, not as I will, but as you will" (Matthew 26:39 ESV). Trusting in the plan of God for our lives means relinquishing our own will and personal desires even during the difficult times. When asked to obey God's will, by faith we trust that He will provide the strength to do all that He asks of us.

We see Jesus always doing the will of the Father, even in heaven as He always did on earth. "I always do the things that are pleasing to him," said Jesus (John 8:29 ESV).

By example, Jesus taught us to approach Our Father with requests, having the same attitude as He himself had: "Nevertheless, not as I will, but as you will." When we desire God's will to be done not only in our personal lives, but also in our homes so that each loved one in our family on earth might be forever in God's heavenly home, we also pray for God's will to be done by our loved ones, mentioning each one by name.

We pray that His will be done in our church families ... in our neighborhoods ... in our towns and cities ... in all countries throughout the world (1Timothy 2:1-4). We desire that Our Father's plan of salvation might be accepted and obeyed by all who come into our thoughts as we pray. We ask to be filled with eager anticipation as we wait for people to be born again into the family of God. We ask to be watchful for indications of the doing of God's will so that lives and hearts might come into harmony with His will here on earth and into eternity.

We tell Our Father the names of people we know who are lost and not living according to His will. We pray for each one by name, asking that His Spirit might work in their lives so that those mentioned will be born into the family of God.

Filling the Earth and Filling Heaven

When an unhurried period of prayer time is set aside to spend in the pleasure of our Father's company, we may take a moment to think back to Adam and Eve, remembering God's will for them. He said, "Be fruitful and increase in number; fill the earth" (Genesis 1:28 NIV). Adam and Eve were to give birth to children who would one day become husbands and wives who in time would give birth to even more children. Men and women to fill the earth so they might be lavishly loved by the infinite God who is love! More and more people who would love Him!

Before leaving this earth and returning to the heavenly realm, Jesus spoke words similar to what was said to Adam and Eve. This time, however, Jesus instructed His followers to fill heaven!

Jesus commanded, "Go out quickly into the streets and alleys of the town and bring in the poor, the crippled, the blind and the lame.... Go out to the roads and country lanes and make them come in, so that my house will be full" (Luke 14:21, 23 NIV).

And, His final words before He ascended to the right hand of His Father addressed their eternal purpose to fill heaven, "Go and make followers of all people in the world. Baptize them in the name of the Father and the Son and the Holy Spirit. Teach them to obey everything that I have taught you" (Matthew 28:19-20 NCV).

The bridegroom and His bride—living together in harmony and security and living together in a 'one spirit' relationship—desire to become a family! This marriage of love between Christ and each member of His body will bring about a desire for children—new babes, born again, who come into the kingdom because of our union with the bridegroom. The family of God must grow because it is the will of Our Father.

It is Our Father's will that all might be saved and be added to His eternal household. Reading and meditating upon these next words of Jesus, may the desire of each one of us be increased so that our prayer and our will become more like His. May our prayers request God to bring children into His family because of our relationship with Him.

Jesus' Words for Meditation

- "To all who did receive him, to those who believed in his name, he gave the right to become children of God— children born not of natural descent, nor of human decision or a husband's will, but born of God." (John 1:12-13 NIV)

- "For this is the will of My Father, that everyone who looks on the Son and believes in him should have eternal life...." (John 6:40 ESV)

- "...it is not the will of your Father who is in heaven that one of these little ones should perish." (Matthew 18:14 NKJV)

- "I tell you, there is rejoicing in the presence of the angels of God over one sinner who repents." (Luke 15:10 NIV)

- "Jesus answered, 'If people love me, they will obey my teaching. My Father will love them, and we will come to them and make our home with them.'" (John 14:23 NCV)

When the bridegroom, Jesus, and we His bride are united to do the will of Our Father, the family of God will grow in number. Many will become children of God—not born in a physical, earthly way, but born of the water and Spirit (John 3:5-6) according to God's will. While in an attitude of prayer and pausing to think about God's will that His eternal family increase, think about your relatives in Christ. Think about the people Jesus adds to His family calling all 'brother and sister.' Remember that we were all baptized by one Spirit into one body and now we are the body of Christ (1 Corinthians 12:12-27).

In reality, the House of Prayer we have been building is more than a house. It is a home! A household! It is filled with many children of God! There are many brothers and sisters! Our prayers grow to include our family—those who love God and love each other. Together we are a family of people who serve Him and serve each other. As in heaven where angels are servants who do God's will, each of us should look not only to our own interests, but also to the interests of others. Our attitude must be transformed into the same attitude as that of Christ who made himself nothing, taking the very nature of a servant (Philippians 2:4-5:7).

Serving Our Father on earth as the angels serve in heaven, we cling to His promise that we will be successful servants if we do not give up. We may become weary, but Our Father does not want us to stop serving. He wants us to look for opportunities to do good to all people, especially to those who belong to the family of believers (Galatians 6:9-10).

As servants together on earth and in heaven, the family of God—whether men and women or angels—search God's written word so that we will know how people ought to conduct themselves in God's household, which is the church of the living God (1 Timothy 3:15).

Together those on earth and those in heaven continually praise God saying, "I love the house where you live, O Lord, the place where your glory dwells" (Psalm 26:8 NIV).

We love the members of God's household, built on the foundation of the apostles and prophets, with Christ Jesus Himself as the chief cornerstone. In Christ each one of us is a living building block added by Him, growing into a beautiful, spiritual, holy eternal temple. We become the place where God lives by his Spirit (Ephesians 2:19-22).

Loving the house of God means loving those who are our eternal family. We pray for the new birth of those who are not in God's household. We desire that the family may increase on earth and increase in heaven. We continually look forward to a new heaven and a new earth, the home of righteousness (2 Peter 3:13). We long to make our home with Him (John 14:23). We long for our eternal house in heaven, the house built by God (2 Corinthians 5:1).

Our Father has made the down payment on our home in heaven. He has given us His Spirit as a deposit guaranteeing our promised, eternal home (2 Corinthians 5:5; Ephesians 1:13-14).

Our body is our 'home' on earth and the Spirit within us is our down payment—our promise that we have an eternal home in heaven. While we pray and wait for the new heaven and new earth, the everlasting home of righteousness, our goal is to please Our Father on earth as He is pleased in heaven. We make every effort to be found spotless, blameless, and at peace with him (2 Corinthians 5:6-9; 2 Peter 3:14).

While we wait to see our bridegroom face to face, by faith we hold His hand. Together we speak to Our Father, asking that those we love might come into the family of God so that together we might worship in joyful assembly. We pray that we will always eagerly obey His commands so that His will is done in our lives on earth as it is done in the realm of the angels who serve Our Father.

In prayer each one of us says, "Teach me to do your will, for you are my God. Let your good Spirit lead me..." (Psalm 143:10 ESV). And, we know by faith, that God listens to the person who worships Him and does His will (John 9:31). Our Father listens to His Son who stands with us in prayer. His Son always speaks to Him with us. His Son always prays, "Your will be done!"

If we do not try to force our own will, but make our requests— trusting our cares and concerns to His will and His timing—we will surely find rest for our souls (Matthew 11:29). As we trust Our Father, our confidence in approaching Him and asking for what we desire will increase.

Jesus was confident to approach His Father in prayer. Doing the will of God was the spiritual 'food' that sustained and nourished Him throughout His time on earth. He said, "My food is to do the will of him who sent me" (John 4:34 ESV)!

Doing the will of God is food for the nourishment of our souls as much as it was for Jesus'. In order for spirit, soul and body to be kept blameless until Jesus comes again (1 Thessalonians 5:23), the same food that Jesus required while on earth is the very same food we need. We ask for our daily needs because Jesus taught us to pray . . .

Chapter 8

"Give us Today our Daily Bread"
Matthew 6:11

The pleasure of giving and receiving

> "Do not be anxious about anything,
> but in everything by prayer and
> petition, with thanksgiving,
> present your requests to God."
> Philippians 4:6-7 NIV

Giving and receiving draws 'giver' and 'receiver' into closer fellowship, where one gives willingly and joyfully and the other receives with pleasure and gratitude. Sometimes Our Father is the one who gives, and we receive. At other times we give to God, who always loves a cheerful giver (2 Corinthians 9:11). There is mutual pleasure in the exchange of gifts between Our Heavenly Father and His children.

In our House of Prayer as we daily spend time in the pleasure of God's company, we continue to set the desires, wishes, and wants of our hearts within the will of Our Father. We seek to be content in any and every situation (Philippians 4:12). And as we find our contentment in Him, our relationship goes from strength to strength just as He has promised (Psalm 84:1-7).

Even though we try to be content as we are, there will always be physical, emotional, and spiritual needs. We may be gratefully encouraged in the promise that God will meet all our needs (Philippians 4:19), but He desires that we express those needs to Him.

When the followers of Jesus asked Him to teach them to pray, they were instructed to say,

"Give us today our daily bread!"

There is a time to ask for what we need. That time is daily! His will is that we ask for what we need each day of our lives. Physical needs as well as emotional and spiritual needs. When we ask, Our Father will give because everyone who asks receives. Our Father in heaven gives good things to those who ask him (Matthew 7:7, 11).

When Jesus responded to his disciples' request to teach them to pray, he cautioned them against "babbling like the pagans," repeating themselves over and over and over again. He said, "Do not be like them, for your Father knows what you need before you ask him. This, then, is how you should pray... give us today..." (Matthew 6:7-9 NIV). Then He worded a direct request, clear and to the point without groveling, begging or whining.

Our Father does not always give us what we ask the moment we ask it. Occasionally we are surprised with an immediate answer as if He were prepared and waiting until we asked. Most of the time, it seems, we ask and then find ourselves needing to make the same request again the next day. Perhaps we will need to make the same request again next week ...

and maybe even again next year. It is very important, that we keep asking and do not give up. Jesus told a story about a woman who was very persistent in asking a judge for what she needed. She kept asking until she received a positive response and solution to her problem. Jesus told His disciples this story to illustrate that they should always pray and not give up, explaining that people will not always be put off because Our Father will see that they get what they need quickly (Luke 18:1-8).

God already knows what we need which is according to His will. However, too often we do not have because we do not ask or we do not receive because we ask with wrong motives anticipating spending what we get on ourselves and our own pleasures (James 4:2-3).

Each day as we ask Our Father to give us what we need, an interactive communication about our very lives draws us into an ever-deepening relationship. When we ask someone to give us something, the polite response when it is received is, "Thank you!" It shows that we recognize the gift or the favor and that we appreciate what has been done for us. When Our Father gives because we have made a specific request, our faith is strengthened in knowing that our prayer has been heard. We are deeply grateful to Him and must tell Him so.

In addition to giving God our thanks, we tell others about receiving answers to our prayers. As we talk about the answers we receive in response to prayer, our words of joy will encourage more and more people. The people who join with us in thanking God also bring Him glory (2 Corinthians 4:15). Our words telling others of answered prayer are a gift of gratitude to Our Father!

When we ask God to give us what we need, our faith speaks volumes about trusting Him to keep His promises. The more we prayerfully verbalize what we need Him to give us, the more aware we become of all we receive each day. When the blessings He gives cause our cup to overflow (Psalm 23:5), our joy and delight will express itself in our words which overflow from our hearts. We must truly rejoice in the Lord always (Philippians 4:4).

The next time we come to Our Father saying, "Give us," our past experiences with answered prayer will strengthen our faith and produce an attitude of thankfulness even before we receive an answer. The more we praise Him for giving because we have asked, the more we will preface our next requests with words of thanksgiving. The delight we feel when we receive the desires of our hearts will overflow in gratitude every time we speak to Our Father in prayer.

As we focus on the importance of asking God to give us today our daily bread, we know that what He gives we will receive with thanksgiving so that our bodies will be as strong and healthy as possible. God has always been the One—and will always be the only One—who makes grass grow for the cattle, and plants for people to cultivate for their food while living on the earth. God is the One who makes the crops grow that will ultimately give the nourishment, enjoyment, and strength that comes from food (Psalm 104:14-15).

We ask for and receive bread—food that we need for our physical needs. In addition, Our Father gives us bread for our heart—for our emotional, mental, and spiritual needs. This is the kind of bread Jesus spoke about when he said, "It is written: Man shall not live on bread alone, but by every word that comes from the mouth of God" (Deuteronomy 8:3, Matthew 4:4 ESV).

The words of God provide nourishment for our souls. But, just as physical food must be eaten in order for our bodies to receive the benefit, spiritual bread must be read, believed and digested so that we might be spiritually healthy and strong.

Jesus said, "Do not work for food that perishes, but for the food that endures to eternal life, which the Son of Man will give to you" (John 6:27 ESV). When the people heard Jesus say this, they responded, "Sir, give us this bread always" (John 6:34 ESV). Our request will be the same as theirs when we pray,

"Give us today our daily *spiritual* bread."

The promise spoken to them is the very same promise that is ours. Jesus declared, "I am the bread of life. He who comes to me will never go hungry" (John 6:34-35 NIV).

Jesus is our spiritual bread. Every word He spoke, every word His preincarnate Spirit inspired in the Old Testament, every inspired word in the writings of the New Testament, every thought, every chapter and every verse are to become the daily bread for our spiritual survival. We must eat spiritual bread daily all the days that we spend on earth so that we may be "thoroughly equipped for every good work" (2 Timothy 3:17 NKJV).

Pray to give as He gives to me

We ask God to "Give us today our daily bread" and He would remind us by saying, "Give, (and) it will be given to you. Good measure, pressed down, shaken together, running over, will be put into our lap. For with the measure you use, it will be measured to you" (Luke 6:38 ESV).

Living and loving in an eternal relationship, we long to bring God the joy of not only giving to us so that we might receive with thanksgiving; but we desire to give to Him so that He might be pleased. We long to have the mind of Christ who said, "I seek not to please myself, but Him who sent me" (John 5:30 NIV).

Following the example of Jesus who looked not for ways to please Himself, but rather looked for what would please His Father, we also seek to discover what pleases Our Father. There are many wonderful ways we can give to Him! We will be abundantly blessed to give God what pleases Him:

- "The prayer of the upright pleases him."
  (Proverbs 15:8 NIV)

- "I will praise the name of God with a song and magnify him with thanksgiving. This will please the Lord."
  (Psalm 69:30-31 ESV)

- "Beloved, if our heart does not condemn us, we have confidence before God; and whatever we ask we receive from him, because we keep his commandments and do what pleases him. And this is his commandment that we believe in the name of His Son Jesus Christ

and love one another, just as he has commanded us."
(1 John 3:21-23 ESV)

- "… we have not ceased to pray for you, asking that you may be filled with the knowledge of his will in all spiritual wisdom and understanding, so as to walk in a manner worthy of the Lord, fully pleasing to him, bearing fruit in every good work and increasing in the knowledge of God." (Colossians 1:9-10 ESV)

- "We make it our goal to please Him...."
(2 Corinthians 5:9 NIV)

- "…we speak, not to please man, but to please God who tests our hearts." (1 Thessalonians 2:4 ESV)

- "…we instructed you how to live in order to please God, as in fact you are living. Now we ask you and urge you in the Lord Jesus to do this more and more."
(1 Thessalonians 4:1 NIV)

- With faith it is possible to please God!
(Hebrews 11:6 paraphrased by author)

- "Through Him (Jesus) then, let us continually offer up a sacrifice of praise to God, that is, the fruit of lips that give thanks to His name. And do not neglect doing good and sharing, for with such sacrifices God is pleased."
(Hebrews 13:15-16 NASB)

Having the mind of Christ, which is always pleasing to Our Father, will give us a greater awareness of the needs of others for their daily bread. Jesus said, "I have compassion for the people.... I do not want to send them away hungry, for they might faint on the way" (Matthew 15:32 NASB). He gave them bread and fish to satisfy their physical hunger as well as spiritual bread in the words He spoke to them.

With the mind of Christ, let us look around at the people in our circle of influence. May we have the compassion of Christ as we look upon their needs. Many need physical bread. All need spiritual bread.

May we see physical needs and be quick to respond with comfort, encouragement, food, clothes, friendship, or with a helping hand that will fill—within our ability—whatever lack might present itself. When we give to others, we are giving to Jesus and to Our Father (Matthew 25:34-40).

May our depth of compassion become like that of Christ as we look upon people. We must not send them away hungry for the bread of life because they have not been fed the words that come from the mouth of God. May no one faint on the way when we could have done or said something that would have encouraged and strengthened their body and soul.

As we pray for God to increase our faith, we must also ask that He increase our compassion and desire to give. From the many blessings Our Father gives to each of us there will always be enough to share. We have been given much so that can give more (Luke 12:48).

If we have been given good health, there is energy to devote to the needs of others. If we have been given a clear mind, there is the ability to structure our time in order to pray for others. If we have been given work, doing something useful with our own hands, we will have something to share with those in need (Ephesians 4:28).

If we have been given more than enough of the basic needs of life, from the storehouse of bank accounts, kitchen cupboards and clothes closets will come much to help those in need. If we have been given twenty-four hours in each day, there will be time to share ourselves in friendship with the lonely and those who need the kindness of someone who cares. If we have been blessed with the ability to communicate, there will be ways to speak or write the words of Jesus which will bring hope and encouragement to others.

"God loves a cheerful giver," Paul said to the church in Corinth as they gathered money to give to other Christians in need. As we read slowly and think carefully about what Paul wrote (2 Corinthians 9:6-7, 10-15 NIV), we will . . .

- "Remember this: Whoever sows sparingly will also reap sparingly and whoever sows generously will also reap generously.

- "Each of you should give what you have decided in your heart to give, not reluctantly or under compulsion, for God loves a cheerful giver...

- "Now he who supplies seed to the sower and bread for food will also supply and increase your store of seed and will enlarge the harvest of your righteousness.

- "You will be made rich in every way so that you can be generous on every occasion, and your generosity will result in thanksgiving to God.

- "This service that you perform is not only supplying the needs of the Lord's people but is also overflowing in many expressions of thanks to God.

- "Because of the service by which you have proved yourselves, others will praise God for the obedience that accompanies your confession of the gospel of Christ, and for your generosity in sharing with them and with everyone else.

- "And in their prayers for you their hearts will go out to you, because of the surpassing grace God has given you. Thanks be to God for his indescribable gift!"

We ask God to give us our daily bread—both earthly bread and heavenly bread. And, He provides everything we need for life here and into eternity. In return, our gratitude overflows so that we give as He gives. The early Christians were praised because they gave themselves first to the Lord and then to God's family of believers (2 Corinthians 8:5).

The family relationship between Our Father, Jesus our brother, and all those who, including us, are called the 'family of God' brings us together often for the family meal, the sharing of bread together. Like the earliest Christians, we come together on the first day of the week to break bread (Acts 20:7). We meet together weekly—frequently even more often—to motivate one another to love God and each other by doing good things

(Hebrews 10:24-25). Opportunities to encourage one another present themselves when we gather around the Lord's table.

We eat the "true food and drink the true drink," feeding on Jesus himself, the "bread that came down from heaven"— bread that comes with His promise that "whoever feeds on this bread will live forever" (John 6:53-58 NIV).

With thanksgiving we present our needs to God (Philippians 4:6) with all kinds of prayers and requests (Ephesians 6:18). We pray for our own needs. We pray for the needs of others. We show our trust and sincere desire to receive what we ask according to His will by our perseverance in prayer. We resolve not to give up praying.

Our prayer requests often present to God our disappointments, fears, deep concerns, hard decisions—those things where we desire His superior wisdom, intervention and action; but we don't know exactly how to ask according to His will. We run out of words. Our emotions are intense, but our mouths are dry and our minds unable to formulate the right words. In our relationships with a loving marriage partner, or between parent and child, or in the presence of a dear friend, there are times when we just sit together quietly without words. Perhaps our head will lie upon another's shoulder, our hands touching and tears falling.

Our compassionate God understands these times and asks us to come to Him for comfort and help. He comforts us, telling us that His Spirit understands emotions deep within our hearts. The apostle Paul joins with us through inspired words of encouragement:

> "… we do not know how to pray as we should, but the Spirit Himself intercedes for us with groanings too deep for words; and He who searches the hearts knows what the mind of the Spirit is, because He intercedes for the saints according to the will of God" (Romans 8:26-27 NASB).

When we cannot form our thoughts into prayer requests, the Holy Spirit will speak for us. We may rest our heads against Our Heavenly Father's shoulder knowing that He understands and comforts us while He works toward giving us what we have asked. Even when we cannot form our own words of prayer, we can say a heartfelt, "Thank you, Father" because He is our "Father of compassion and the God of all comfort, who comforts us in all our troubles" (2 Corinthians 1:3-4 NIV).

Trials come and trials go, but they serve a purpose. As our faith is tested, we become stronger. As we receive comfort and compassion from Our Father, our love for Him draws us into a deeper, more intimate relationship.

God wants us to persevere "so that we will be mature and complete, not lacking in anything" (James 1:2-4 NIV). But sometimes we grow weary. We withdraw from Him and seek to take care of our needs by ourselves. Rather than asking Him, we simply push forward in our own strength to try to solve our problems and take care of our own desires. We begin to trust more in ourselves and less in Him. There seems to be no time for our relationship, no time for prayer, and no place in our busy lives to enjoy the pleasure of His company.

Oh, how we need to pray . . .

Chapter 9

"Forgive Us Our Sins"
Matthew 6:12, Luke 11:4

The pleasure of a loving relationship when we are wrong

> "I will be careful to lead
> a blameless life.
> When will you come to me?
> I will conduct the affairs
> of my house
> with a blameless heart."
> Psalm 101:2 NIV

Careful to lead a life that is blameless! Sinless! Forgiven! Why? Because Jesus *will* come *to me!* He will come to me on *the* last day. On the last day when Jesus comes, I will either be among those who are dead in Christ, my life on earth finished before His coming; or, I will be among those "who are still alive and are left." If He comes while I am alive, I will join those who "will be caught up together... to meet the Lord in the air. And so we will be with the Lord forever" (1 Thessalonians 4:16-17 ESV).

Yes! He *will* come! It is a promise! Jesus' last recorded words of promise are, "Yes, I am coming soon" (Revelation 22:20 NIV)!

We sometimes wonder, "How soon is *soon*, Lord? It has now been so very long since You said You were coming "soon."

Our encouragement comes from the inspired words of the prophet Habakkuk. He longed for the fulfillment of prophecy and for the coming of Messiah many years before Jesus was born in Bethlehem. Our Father's words spoken long ago reveal His eternal nature and serve as encouragement to us now:

> "For the revelation awaits an appointed time;
> it speaks of the end and will not prove false.
> Though it linger, wait for it;
> it will certainly come and will not delay."
> Habakkuk 2:3 NIV

When will Jesus "descend from heaven, with a shout and with the trumpet call of God" (1 Thessalonians 4:16 NASB)? I don't know! No one knows except Our Father. We only know until that day we must be careful to lead a blameless life (Psalm 101:2). While we are waiting, we must be diligent to be found without a spot of sin, blameless and at peace with him (2 Peter 3:13-14).

Sometimes when we are praying, it feels like God is very far away; and we may wonder if He even hears us. One reason for this sense of separation might possibly be because our sins have separated us from Our Father. Our unrepented sins will cause Him to turn His face from us so as not to hear us (Isaiah 59:1-2).

The House of Prayer where God and I enjoy the pleasure of each other's company must contain no sin because sin will cause Our Father to cover Himself with a cloud so that no prayer can get through (Lamentations 3:44). The words "forgive me" must be spoken sincerely so that God may once again make us blameless in His sight.

And then, blameless in Our Father's presence, our hearts will not condemn us so that we can have confidence before Him. Whatever we ask we receive from Him, because we obey His commands and do what pleases Him (1 John 3:21-22). We will continue to pray and live as we have promised, doing His will on earth as it is done in heaven.

Doing what pleases Our Father as well as trying to please the others in our lives—those who need our daily care and attention—brings many responsibilities. It also brings many opportunities to do good; however, doing good can, and frequently does, become very time consuming. The time spent in prayer, which we recognize as so important, often is set aside because of the genuine demands that crowd out our good intentions. An ongoing list of 'Things to Do' frequently takes away any plan we had to pray and to feed upon the word of God.

Each time we become too busy or too absorbed in our own lives, Jesus will begin knocking upon the door of our thoughts, trying to get our attention. He comes to tell us it is time to make a change. As He knocks, Jesus has with Him all the grace-filled mercy and forgiveness we need. Perhaps as we examine ourselves, the reason there is not enough time to pray is not really a matter of being too busy, but rather a matter of unresolved sin. The real truth may be that we have been avoiding the intimacy of prayer because our sin is present and we are being slow to take a stand against it.

When Jesus knocks, He says, "Those whom I love I rebuke and discipline. So be earnest, and repent. Here I am! I stand at the door and knock. If anyone hears my voice and opens the door, I will come in and eat with that person and they with me" (Revelation 3:19-20 NIV).

Jesus knocks to invite us once again into the pleasure of His Father's company. He invites us again because He loves us! When we grow negligent and let days, even weeks pass without spending quality time with Jesus at Our Father's throne, the door slowly drifts closed. Perhaps, not slamming . . . just gently closing between us. At times like this, if asked, we would say, "Yes, of course, I still love God, but I just have no time." How can there be no time for Our Father and His Son? If we were to spend no time with our loved ones and friends, soon we would drift apart. Relationships would suffer. Our relationship with God suffers in the same way when we do not set aside time to spend with Him.

As Jesus stands knocking, trying to get our attention, He says, "Repent. Open the door. Hear my voice. Let us feast together on the words of God."

When we hear His voice and feel remorse for allowing our times of prayer and meditation on His word to become neglected, He is always eager for us to begin anew. God is never too busy to spend time with us. The door can be opened to Him and we may say, "Come in Lord. Search me. Look into my heart. Test me. See my anxious thoughts. See if there is anything in me that causes you grief. Lead me on the way of everlasting life" (Psalm 139:23-24).

Once again, and yet again and again, we may open ourselves to the pleasure of His company through daily prayer, repenting of any sin we have allowed to enter and block our prayers. God's word encourages us to rejoice because each one of us may say,

> "If I had cherished sin in my heart, the Lord would not have listened; but God has surely listened and has heard my prayer. Praise be to God, who has not rejected my prayer or withheld his love from me" (Psalm 66:18-20 NIV).

As we reflect upon having said, "Give us today our daily bread," we know how abundantly blessed we are. Daily we see His blessings being showered upon us. We are filled with heartfelt gratitude. We desire that nothing come between us and the wonderful pleasure of Our Father's company.

When sin and neglect have kept us from enjoying the pleasure of prayer, we may rejoice in all humility and with deep gratitude knowing that "God shows his love for us in that while we were still sinners, Christ died for us" (Romans 5:8 ESV). His forgiveness is waiting for us. Our Father is waiting for us to say, "Please, Father, do not let us fade and dry up like autumn leaves and blow away in the wind" (Isaiah 64:6). Gather us! Gather our thoughts and priorities like raking leaves which have fallen to the ground! Gather our thoughts and priorities so that we may praise You for the wonderful free gift of eternal life in Christ Jesus our Lord (Romans 6:23).

We ask Our Father to reveal areas in our life that are not pleasing to Him so that we can confess our sins and repent. We also ask Our Father to reveal to us what kind of people we ought to be as we wait for the coming of Jesus (2 Peter 3:11). Words spoken from our heart tell Him that we desire to live holy and godly lives. We pray,

"Forgive us our sins."

As we pray, "Forgive us our sins," it is so important to be very specific in describing our sin or sins. For example we read:

> "…the cowardly, the unbelieving, the vile, the murderers, the sexually immoral, those who practice magic arts, the idolaters and all liars— they will be consigned to the fiery lake of burning sulfur." (Revelation 21:8 NIV)

Reading God's words here and in other scriptures, we may recognize our own sins. It is then that we must pray very specifically. Perhaps we have been cowardly to share our faith with others. We could then pray, "Please forgive me for being a coward. I was embarrassed to speak about You when I had the perfect opportunity."

Maybe we have stopped praying because we are refusing to believe, thinking there is no possible way that a certain problem can be solved.

Our words may have used God's name in a vile and disrespectful way.

Gossip may have murdered another's reputation or stolen their privacy.

Thinking what we are doing is 'just for fun,' perhaps we have experimented with the magic arts.

Idolatry—greed for the things of this world—may be the reason we are too busy to spend time with God.

Our lies may have deceived and hurt others.

In an attitude of mournful, sincere repentance, we define our sin in specific terms. When was it done? How did it offend God? Did it harm someone else? Then, we pray very specifically to Our Father, requesting, "Please forgive me because I _____." We state in our prayer of confession the exact details of our sin.

After asking Our Father to forgive us and make us blameless in His sight, we pause in prayer to see with eyes of faith. We see Jesus on the cross. We visualize Christ, the One who had no sin, becoming sin for us so that in Him we might become the righteousness of God (2 Corinthians 5:21). By faith we meditate upon our sin visualizing it being removed from us and placed upon Jesus as He hangs on the cross. With a sense of sadness and gratitude blended together, we let ourselves enjoy the pleasure of being in the company of our brother, and friend, and Savior who loved us and made Himself a substitute for our sin (Ephesians 5:2).

Now, we rejoice to claim His promise that "if we confess our sins, he is faithful and just to forgive us our sins and cleanse us from all unrighteousness" (1 John 1:9 ESV). We see ourselves pure and blameless. We grasp the reality that at this moment in time and in this blameless relationship we are ready for Jesus to come!

As we continue praying, with our thoughts still focused upon "Forgive us our sins," we ask God to reveal, forgive and remove the sins in our lives that we do not yet fully recognize or understand. We ask Him to prepare us so that we will be quick to repent and confess whatever would hurt our eternal relationship of purity. We pray the inspired words of the psalmist:

> "Forgive my hidden faults.
> Keep your servant also from willful sins;
> may they not rule over me.
> Then will I be blameless,
> innocent of great transgression."
> Psalm 19:12-13 NIV

While pausing in prayer to rejoice in the forgiveness Our Father has given, we should now consider whether or not our sin has hurt someone else—someone other than God. Each one of us must ask ourselves, "Have I given everyone what I owe? Is there a debt I owe that remains outstanding (Romans 13:8)? Have I done harm to my neighbor (Romans 13:10)?"

The Spirit of God may reveal that the outstanding debt we owe is a sincere apology. We may very well need to seek the forgiveness of a certain person. Many times there are things we do or say, or don't do and don't say, that need to be made right.

Words that express how sorry we are need to be spoken to the one our actions or words have hurt. As we come to Our Father in prayer and remember that someone has something against us (Matthew 5:23), it will please Our Father if we pause our prayer long enough to go immediately to settle the matter and be reconciled if possible (Matthew 5:24-25). And then, we return to our prayer. Forgiveness is sought from the people in our lives to whom we owe an apology. This needs to be done while they are still with us (Matthew 5:25). Matters need to be settled quickly before it is too late.

When seeking the forgiveness of someone against whom we have sinned, wisdom from God must become one of our prayer requests. If we want to acknowledge that we have sinned against someone, but this person is not aware of our secret thoughts or hidden motives, perhaps the wise thing to do is to make our confession only to God. We should be very careful that the person to whom we give our apology already knows how we have sinned against them. Sometimes the desire to make things right, can make things worse if the person was not aware of how we secretly felt toward them.

One day Jesus invited himself to the home of a despised tax collector, a man the crowds called 'a sinner.' This man opened his door to Jesus and welcomed Him gladly. The man's name was Zacchaeus. He was a small man with big sins. In the presence of Jesus, Zacchaeus became convicted of his sins. Not only did he need the forgiveness that would make him blameless in the eyes of God, he wanted to take action and do what he could to make things right with those against whom he had sinned.

Zacchaeus said to Jesus, "Look, Lord! I give half of my goods to the poor; and if I have taken anything from anyone by false accusation, I restore fourfold" (Luke 19:8 NKJV).

Jesus rejoiced and said to Zacchaeus, "Today salvation has come to this house" (Luke 19:9). Salvation expressing itself through forgiveness comes to us daily as we continually repent and confess our sins. His grace continually purifies us (1 John 1:7), making us blameless in Our Father's sight. Zacchaeus felt deep joy and gratitude as he found himself acceptable in the sight of God. And, so do we.!

We too will desire to say 'Thank you' over and over again to Our Father and to our Savior Jesus, 'Thank you' because we are "the blessed whose sins are forgiven, whose wrongs are pardoned, whom the Lord does not consider guilty" (Romans 4:7-8 NCV).

Sometimes a particular past sin or many sins—even though forgiven—will plague our thoughts. Our Father's words will always encourage us every time we come to Him with the memory of past sins. His words will speak to us saying, "There is now no condemnation for those who are in Christ Jesus" (Romans 8:1 NASB).

His words will also remind us to forget what is past. Let the past go. Press forward toward our eternal goal (Philippians 3:13-14). Forget what happened before, and do not think about the past (Isaiah 43:18-19 NCV).

Rejoicing in prayer, we praise His name saying, "Hallowed be your name because you are called 'I AM the LORD Who Makes You Holy'" (Leviticus 20:7-8 NIV).

We rejoice because He is able to keep us from stumbling. He is the one who is able to make us stand blameless and with great joy in the presence of His glory (Jude 24 NASB).

Our Father's love prepared forgiveness for us in His mind before the world was created. Jesus prepared for the forgiveness of our sins—yours and mine—long before we were born. With a truly repentant heart and lips that confess our sin, forgiveness is waiting for each person who longs to be blameless in the pleasure of His company.

As our prayer continues, the question to ask might be, "Does gratitude for our own forgiveness bring about a desire to be imitators of God (Ephesians 5:1)?"

Are we as prepared to forgive as He is?

Are we ready to pray, "Forgive us our sins . . .

Chapter 10

꒰꒡꒱

"As We Also Forgive Everyone Who Sins Against Us"
Luke 11:4

The pleasure of a loving relationship when we are right

> "Do to others as you would
> have them do to you."
> Luke 11:31 NIV

orgiven! It's what we desire to be! We long for Our Father's continual forgiveness. We repent and confess our sins knowing that the Father—because of His Son's perfect life and sacrificial death upon the cross—is continually prepared to forgive. He is faithful to forgive us and to cleanse us of all unrighteousness (1 John 1:9). As we grow in our desire to please Him, we realize how abundant His supply of forgiveness is.

How wonderful it is to be purified of all unrighteousness. In Him! Forgiven! We become righteous in Him! Our prayers become "powerful and effective" (James 5:16 NIV). In our House of Prayer we continue to find delight in the pleasure of Our

Father's company. We ask according to His will and He stands ready to respond. We ask to be forgiven. He forgives!

We say the words Jesus taught us to pray,

"Forgive us our sins, as we forgive everyone who sins against us"

By verbalizing these words, "Forgive us our sins, as we forgive everyone who sins against us," we tell Him that we desire to walk by the Spirit as Jesus did (Galatians 5:16). We reaffirm that our desire is to walk through life imitating Him by forgiving others.

We express our desire to obey His command to "be imitators of God as beloved children and live a life of love, as Christ loved us and gave himself up for us" (Ephesians 5:1-2 ESV).

Our Father has asked us to forgive, knowing that when we forgive, we understand to an even greater degree what it cost Him to forgive us. It is seldom easy to forgive someone who has hurt us deeply. It's not easy to forgive before we receive a sincere apology, but we must prepare ourselves in advance as God prepared in advance for the forgiveness of all men and women.

> "God shows his love for us in that while we
> were still sinners, Christ died for us."
> Romans 5:8 ESV

Yes, we desire to receive our Father's forgiveness. And, we want to be forgiven by others when we come to them with our sincere apology. Jesus said, "Do to others as you would have them do to you" (Luke 6:31 NIV). When we go to someone to ask forgiveness for what we have done or said, we hope they will have a heart that forgives. Because we ourselves desire to be forgiven, we prepare ourselves to forgive those who need to seek our forgiveness. Our prayer is that we might forgive others as we would have them forgive us. We listen to and heed Jesus' warnings:

> "For if you forgive other people when they sin against you, your heavenly Father will also forgive you. But if you do not forgive others their sins, your Father will not forgive your sins" (Matthew 6:14 NIV).

We imitate Jesus and give ourselves up as He gave Himself up for us. We give up any rights we might think we have to retaliate against the one who has sinned against us. As we ask Our Father, "Please forgive us our sins as we forgive everyone who sins against us," the Word of God says to us:

> "Beloved, never avenge yourselves, but leave it to the wrath of God, for it is written, 'Vengeance is mine, I will repay, says the Lord.' To the contrary, if your enemy is hungry, feed him; if he is thirsty, give him something to drink; for by so doing you will heap burning coals on his head. Do not be overcome by evil, but overcome evil with good" (Romans 12:19-21 ESV).

Being overcome by evil seems a dismal prospect as a result of bitterness and anger against someone who has hurt us. Clinging to the hope of revenge is not an option for those who desire to have their prayers heard by God and who desire to live blameless until His coming. Being forgiven much by Our Father and then being unwilling to forgive someone who has wronged us brings terrible consequences.

One day Jesus told a story, called a parable, to teach His followers how Our Father in heaven will treat each of us unless we forgive others:

> "The kingdom of heaven is like a king who wanted to settle accounts with his servants. As he began the settlement, a man who owed him ten thousand bags of gold was brought to him. Since he was not able to pay, the master ordered that he and his wife and his children and all that he had be sold to repay the debt.

> "The servant fell on his knees before him. 'Be patient with me,' he begged, 'and I will pay back everything.' The servant's master took pity on him, canceled the debt and let him go.

> "But when that servant went out, he found one of his fellow servants who owed him a hundred silver coins. He grabbed him and began to choke him. 'Pay back what you owe me!' he demanded.

> "His fellow servant fell to his knees and begged him, 'Be patient with me, and I will pay you back.'

"But he refused. Instead, he went off and had the man thrown into prison until he could pay the debt. When the other servants saw what had happened, they were greatly distressed and went and told their master everything that had happened.

"Then the master called the servant in. 'You wicked servant,' he said, 'I canceled all that debt of yours because you begged me to. Shouldn't you have had mercy on your fellow servant just as I had on you?' In anger his master <u>handed him over to the jailers to be tortured</u>, until he should pay back all he owed.

"This is how my heavenly Father will treat each of you unless you forgive your brother from your heart" (Matthew 18:23-35 NIV underlined emphasis by author).

Our Heavenly Father has forgiven us so much. To those of us with repentant hearts He is available to hear our confession of sin whenever we come through Jesus directly to Him in prayer. His great love and tender mercy removes the huge debt we owe Him. He sends us on our way rejoicing and free from guilt! Freed from eternal death!

But, as we travel on the road toward our eternal home, we pass many going in the opposite direction. We meet people who are "lovers of themselves, lovers of money, boasters, proud, blasphemers, disobedient to parents, unthankful, unholy, unloving, unforgiving, slanderers, without self-control, brutal, despisers of good, traitors, headstrong, haughty, lovers of pleasure rather than lovers of God" (2 Timothy 3:1-5 NKJV).

Even though we try to have nothing to do with them (2 Timothy 3:5), they may have much to do with us: The husband or wife who changed into a different person from the one we married. The precious child we reared who became an adult with a character far from the one we sought to instill. Parents who don't understand our faith. Co-workers who have their own agendas. Those who once called us friends. Governments. Many people and circumstances along our way. In a world filled with those who are not 'lovers of God'—and sadly even in the family of God—there will be abuses, insults, and sin committed against us. How we deal with these offenses will determine whether we continue on our way trusting in Our Father, hand in hand with Jesus our Lord, or whether our Lord and Master hands us over to be tortured.

If we do not forgive everyone who sins against us, we will find ourselves imprisoned by the most destructive of emotions. Recurring memories of sins against us will torture us. Anger may continue to burn within us. We may be quick to take offense and lash out in return, saying and doing things that we would never have done or said if we were willing to follow God's command to forgive. When we retell the story of the person who sinned against us, the events and circumstances can become worse with each telling. We may even look for ways to hurt the one who has hurt us. We contemplate the possibility of revenge. When the hurt does not go away and there seems no way to resolve the conflict, depression frequently slams the doors of our mind into a very tight lock down.

The key to freedom from this kind of unbearable jail is 'forgiveness.' Our Father asks us to forgive so that "no advantage would be taken of us by Satan, for we are not ignorant of his schemes" (2 Corinthians 2:11 NASB). Satan is a cruel jailer who is happy to torture believer and non-believer in his prison. We are trapped in his prison of torture until we are ready to . . .

> "Get rid of all bitterness, rage and anger, brawling and slander, along with every form of malice. Be kind and compassionate to one another, forgiving each other, just as in Christ, God forgave you" (Ephesians 4:31-32 NIV).

As long as we are not careful to forgive as we have been forgiven, the light of Jesus within us is in danger of becoming darkness (Luke 11:35).

The door of disappointment and victimization—the door to the jail where a person is tortured by bitterness and all its companions—will open when we forgive everyone who sins against us. 'Forgiveness' truly is the key. When we use the key, Our Father unlocks the door. We release to Him what is His alone—revenge! When a person sins against another, God is the only one who must judge and punish. Not us!

In prayer we give everyone who has sinned against us into the hands of God who is the judge of all mankind and to Jesus who is the mediator–the advocate and lawyer (Hebrews 12:23-24).

If it is possible to go to the one who has sinned against us, having prepared ourselves to forgive, we go to that person and show them their fault, just between the two of us. If that person listens to us, we have achieved an important first step toward healing the relationship (Matthew 18:15). This is the most ideal of circumstances and what each one of us would pray to happen. And if that person who sinned against us, sins against us again, we might question along with the apostle Peter, "Lord, how often shall my brother sin against me, and I forgive him? Up to seven times?"

"I tell you not seven times, but seventy times seven," is Jesus' reply (Matthew 18:21-23 NKJV). He instructs that we continue to forgive as long as we need God's forgiveness!

When we forgive by placing the one who has hurt us into the hands of God for punishment or revenge, we uproot bitterness and all its accompanying emotional pain. The tenderness of God responds to each one of us when we are the victim of sin. When a decision is not made to rid ourselves of all those emotions that torture us when we harbor a grudge and refuse to forgive, our sin of withholding forgiveness will require repentance and confession.

"For when I kept silent, my bones wasted away through my groaning all day long. For day and night your hand was heavy upon me; my strength was dried up as by the heat of summer. I acknowledged my sin to you, and I did not cover my iniquity; I said, 'I will confess my transgressions to the LORD,' and you forgave the iniquity of my sin. Therefore let everyone who is godly offer prayer to you at a time when you may be found" (Psalm 32:3-6 ESV).

When we stop torturing ourselves with negative, destructive thoughts and actions against everyone who sins against us, Jesus draws us near to Himself once again and in His presence we reach out our hand and reaffirm,

"I am continually with you;
you hold my right hand.
You guide me with your counsel,
and afterward you will receive me to glory.
Whom have I in heaven but you?
And there is nothing on earth that I desire besides you.
My flesh and my heart may fail,
but God is the strength of my heart and my portion forever.
For behold, those who are far from you shall perish;
you put an end to everyone who is unfaithful to you.
But for me it is good to be near God!"
Psalm 73:23-28 ESV

As we walk hand in hand with Jesus, He would remind us to always "Give to everyone what you owe him" (Romans 13:7 NIV). If we owe forgiveness, we give forgiveness! He would continue, "Love does no harm to its neighbor" (Romans 13:10 NKJV). We will be encouraged, knowing because of His forgiveness, we have found the courage and resolve to forgive rather than to harm the one who has hurt us.

But, we ask, "What if someone sins against me and I go to this person to try to be reconciled and they refuse to listen? What if there is no desire on their part to apologize or accept responsibility for their own wrongful actions? What if I am met with resistance and anger?"

Jesus said, "Treat him as you would a heathen" (Matthew 18:17 NKJV). Treat the one who does not ask for, nor want our forgiveness like a heathen ... a nonbeliever ... an ungodly person. Remember, however, Christ died for the ungodly (Romans 5:6)! Through careful and specific prayer, our attitude toward the ungodly person in our life will become more like Christ's. Even though it is difficult to think of the one who has sinned against us in a positive way, God promises us success so that we may rejoice in hope, saying, "I can do all things through Christ who strengthens me" (Philippians 4:13 NKJV).

Remembering to be imitators of Christ, we prayerfully prepare our forgiveness in advance just as Our Father demonstrated His love for us in that "while we were still sinners Christ died for us" (Romans 5:8 ESV). While those who have sinned against us may remain hardened, we prepare ourselves for how we will think about them and how we will treat them until the day they do ask our forgiveness. All the while we understand that day may never come. But as long as they live and as long as we live, our attitude must be one of forgiveness. We give everyone who sins against us and does not ask our forgiveness into the hands of God. We give up our desire to seek revenge and retribution. We request in prayer that our mind will be set with the same attitude as that of Christ Jesus (Philippians 2:5): Forgiving as He has forgiven!

Our attitude will then become the attitude of Christ who said, "Father, forgive them for they do not know what they are doing" (Luke 23:44 NASB). We begin to pray for our enemies, not because we feel a warmth of affection for the one who has hurt us, but because it's what God wants. We decide to forgive just as we decide to love. We don't wait for the right emotions to enter our hearts. Nor do we wait for the one who sinned against us to beg our forgiveness.

We are motivated by the will of God to love and to forgive, because Jesus has commanded everyone to . . .

- Love your enemies
- Do good to those who hate you
- Bless those who curse you
- Pray for those who spitefully use you
- Be merciful, as your Father also is merciful
- Judge not
- Condemn not
- Forgive, and you will be forgiven

(Luke 6:27-37)

Daily we continue to pray for God's help to love as He loves. Thinking about the one who has sinned against us, we pray for strength and resolve . . .

- To be patient
- To be kind
- Not to envy
- Not to boast
- Not to be proud
- Not to be rude
- Not to be self-seeking
- Not to be easily angered
- To keep no record of wrongs
- Not to delight in evil
- To rejoice with the truth
- To protect
- To trust
- To hope
- To persevere
- To believe that 'Love never fails!'

(1 Corinthians 13:4-8)

Remember, God's kindness is meant to lead us all to repentance (Romans 2:4b). His kindness did lead those of us who dwell in His House of Prayer to repentance. Now we are in His very presence because we are forgiven. When God's qualities of love and kindness are seen in us, the one who has sinned against us may very well be led to repentance.

Forgiven and forgiving others, we are led by God to beautiful green pastures and quiet waters, where He restores our souls and guides us in paths of righteousness (Psalm 23:2-3). In this peaceful quiet setting—free from bitterness and anger—it would be wonderful if we could linger awhile longer to enjoy the heavenly pleasure of His company without moving forward in our prayer thoughts.

However, reflecting upon the reality that in the future we will be harassed by problems and suffering, we must now prayerfully seek His protection. We may feel weak in the face of future temptation and the realization that we will sin again. Not wanting this feeling of weakness to immobilize us, we sincerely empathize with the apostle Paul who shared what Our Father revealed to him, "My grace is sufficient for you, for my power is made perfect in weakness."

And with Paul we will continue to say, "Therefore I will boast all the more gladly about my weaknesses, so that the power of Christ may rest on me. For the sake of Christ, then, I am content with weaknesses, insults, hardships, persecutions, and calamities. For when I am weak, then I am strong" (2 Corinthians 12: 9-10 ESV).

And we will pray fervently . . .

Chapter 11

"Lead Us Not Into Temptation"
Matthew 6:13, Luke 11:4b

The pleasure of facing outside pressures together

> "Keep watching and praying
> that you may not enter into temptation."
> Matthew 26:41 NASB

Prayer and praise to Our Father in heaven brings us into His merciful presence. In His presence we rejoice that even though for a little while because of sin in our lives He may have been angry, His anger does not last forever (Isaiah 12:1-2; Jeremiah 3:12). His loving grace and mercy surround us every moment of every day of our lives in Him!

His comforting forgiveness strengthens us and puts a song in our hearts. Having accepted His gracious invitation to enjoy the pleasure of His company, we find our delight in Him knowing that Our Father will give us the desires of our hearts (Psalm 37:4). Our sincere desire is that we never again feel the burden of guilt that comes from a cherished or unconfessed sin. And, yet, we know that as long as we live, we will continue to be tempted to sin. Our spirit is willing to say 'No' to every temptation that would lead us into sin, but weakness of flesh and will is part of our fallen human nature inherited from Adam and Eve.

In prayer, we make a request of Our Father:

> "Do not let my heart be drawn to what is evil so
> that I take part in wicked deeds along with those
> who are evil doers...."
> (Psalm 141:4 NIV)

And, we also expand our prayer asking that He not only give us wings like eagles to rise above our temptations (Isaiah 40:31), but also give us the eyes of an eagle in order to see danger from a heavenly perspective. When we recognize temptation through careful observation, immediately we must speak to Our Father so we might draw upon His strength and wisdom.

Not only do we pray, "Lead us not into this temptation," we earnestly request, *"Lead us away from temptation!"*

Jesus was led by the Spirit into the desert to be tempted by the devil (Matthew 4:1). And then, for the remainder of the three and a half years of His life until His death on the cross, Jesus was "tempted in every way, just as we are—yet he did not sin" (Hebrews 4:15 NIV).

When He taught His followers to pray, "Lead us not into temptation," Jesus had already experienced great suffering from temptation while He was in the desert. Our loving Jesus opens through prayer our source of powerful and effective protection. The power that raised Him from the dead is the same power that can—and will!—help us turn temptation into victory instead of sin. Jesus knew temptation from personal experience. He knew the suffering that accompanies a person's struggle to resist the emotional and physical pull toward sin. Jesus was made of flesh and blood just like us. Because Jesus suffered when He was tempted, He is able to help us when we are being tempted (Hebrews 2:14, 18).

Even though He is God, Jesus, the eternal Word in human flesh, shared in our weaknesses. He knows the difficulty of overcoming temptation. He fervently prayed often for strength from His Father, and He always received the strength needed to resist. He can, and will help us resist. His assistance begins with the warning to "watch and pray so that you will not fall into temptation" (Matthew 26:41 NIV).

On the night before His death, Jesus went out as He had at other times to the Mount of Olives, and His disciples followed Him (Luke 22:39 NIV). He and His disciples had eaten the Passover supper together earlier that evening. Jesus had discussed many things about His death and His departure from them. Then as He reached the garden of Gethsemane on the Mount of Olives, He began to be sorrowful and troubled and He said to them, "My soul is overwhelmed with sorrow to the point of death. Stay here and keep watch with me" (Matthew 26:36-38 NIV).

Then "when he rose from prayer and went back to the disciples, he found them asleep, exhausted from sorrow" (Luke 22:45 NIV).

"'Why are you sleeping,' he asked them. 'Get up and pray so that you will not fall into temptation'" (Luke 22:46 NIV).

Like Jesus' disciples who were exhausted from sorrow, there are times when our own heartache and distress threatens to overpower us. Some of us long for sleep in order to escape the pain that comes from disappointment, fear, and problems that seem insurmountable. While Jesus prayed, His apostles in their emotional exhaustion slept. When He found them sleeping instead of obeying His desire for them to pray while He Himself was in prayer, Jesus exhorted them as He would exhort us, "Get up and pray so that you will not fall into temptation" (Luke 22:40 NIV).

When the longing to escape into sleep overcomes the conviction within you to pray, it's time to force yourself to get up. Wash your face with cold water. Swing your arms to get the blood flowing. Stand instead of sit. Perhaps even walk and pray so that you do not fall asleep.

When in anguish, just as Jesus prayed, we must pray even more earnestly to do the will of Our Father. Jesus' momentary temptation to forsake God's eternal plan of salvation—not to go to the cross and not to take the punishment for the sins of the world upon Himself—was expressed to His Father when He said, "May this cup be taken from me" (Matthew 26:39, 42 NIV). His victory over this temptation came in the next breath when He prayed the desire of His heart, "Yet not as I will, but as you will" (Matthew 26:39, 42 NIV).

Victory over temptation will come to each of us as we seek the will of Our Father. When our desire is to give up or give in to the enticement that would lead us to sin and do the easy thing rather than the will of God, we must pray immediately. Each one of us must tell Our Father, "The desire of my heart is to resist this temptation." We must pray fervently to follow in His steps.

Christ suffered for all of us and gave us an example to follow: He committed no sin (1 Peter 2:21-22)! Any temptation that might come to us is common to everyone. Jesus, as a man, suffered and struggled with every temptation that has come or will ever come to each of us. When we follow His example, doing the will of Our Father, victory will be ours. Just as the apostles were exhorted to watch and pray, we are also warned to be careful.

None of us need to fall into sin. Our Father promises there will always be a way of escape:

> "If you think you are strong, you should be careful not to fall. The only temptation that has come to you is that which everyone has. But you can trust God, who will not permit you to be tempted more than you can stand. But when you are tempted, he will also give you a way to escape so that you will be able to stand it" (1 Corinthians 10:12-13 NCV).

While spending time in prayer with Our Father in heaven, we must stay awake and continue to pray about all things. There will be times when we run out of words. That's the time to pause and take a deep breath. That's the time to pause to meditate. When we are praying about the possibility of present or future temptation, we need to pause in order to bring to mind any specific temptations that might be pursuing us. We examine each temptation, searching God's word to understand His will so that we might respond in a victorious manner. We claim His promise to give us a way to escape—a way out—so we can turn away from our temptation. We ask that He show us the escape route. As we meditate upon His promise to lead us out of temptation, we visualize ourselves standing victorious in Jesus. Strength is received from our Savior—the One who has saved us from all past sin—who will lead us out of temptation and save us from present and future sin.

We listen to the words of Jesus, whose very name means "He will save his people from their sins" (Matthew 1:21). We search His words, knowing and trusting that He guides us with His counsel and advice (Psalm 73:23-24). The Word of God—the spiritual bread that strengthens us and for which we have prayed—becomes our way out of every temptation.

Each morning as we awaken, we know that this day will have its own problems. We find encouragement for each day in the promise that God will give us His power when we are weak (2 Corinthians 12:9-10). Our strength will continue to come from Him so that we might be able to do everything (Philippians 4:13), even to put temptation aside and refuse to sin. We praise Our Father in prayer because we trust that, as He has promised, He will meet all our needs according to His glorious riches in Christ Jesus (Philippians 4:19). When we need a way of escape from temptation, He will meet our need!

We will always have temptations as long as we live, but His strength has been, is, and always will be available to us as we find our delight in Him. His words will always tell us what to do, what to think, and where to go to find the way to escape temptation.

Jesus is our constant traveling companion. He leads. We follow. He is our Shepherd. We are His sheep. He knows our voice as we call upon Him. And, because we are daily feeding upon His words—our spiritual bread—we know His voice (John 10:3-4, 14).

Jesus speaks and we hear Him as we read His words. Our Shepherd is more than sympathetic. He empathizes with our weaknesses because He was tempted in every way, just as we are.

Even though we walk hand in hand with our Shepherd Jesus, temptation is certain to come at every bend in the road and at every crossroad. Sin will try to lure us from our "knowledge of the truth that leads to godliness" (Titus 1:1 NIV). Even though "the highway of the upright turns aside from evil" (Proverbs 16:17 ESV), we will continue to watch and pray so as not to follow any detour that would lead us into temptation. Our spirit is willing to follow Jesus, but our body is weak (Matthew 26:41). As we vigilantly watch along life's journey, we continually pray:

→ "Direct my footsteps according to your word; let no sin rule over me." (Psalm 119:133 NIV)

→ "Lead me in the path of your commands, because that makes me happy. Make me want to keep your rules instead of wishing for riches. Keep me from looking at worthless things. Let me live by your word." (Psalm 119:35-37 NCV)

→ "Lead me, O LORD, in your righteousness because of my enemies–make straight your way before me." (Psalm 5:8 ESV)

→ "Teach me your way, O LORD; lead me on a level path because of my enemies." (Psalm 27:11 ESV)

→ "See if there is any bad thing in me. Lead me on the road to everlasting life." (Psalm 139:24 NCV)

→ "Teach me to do your will, for you are my God! Let your good Spirit lead me on level ground." (Psalm 143:10 ESV)

Praying and watching for temptation—praying and carefully looking for dangers along the way—we must be alert in order to know where to be especially careful. We look for enemies all along the way, knowing that sin will attempt to deceive us. By observation and watchful prayer, we can, and must be prepared.

Sinful enticements that would lure us into leaving the will of Our Father wait to attack in four major places:

1) MYSELF: "Let no one say when he is tempted, 'I am being tempted by God,' for God cannot be tempted with evil, and he himself tempts no one. But each person is tempted when he is lured and enticed by his own desire. Then desire when it has conceived gives birth to sin, and sin when it is fully grown brings forth death." (James 1:13-15 ESV)

2) COMPANIONS: "Brothers and sisters, if someone is caught in a sin, you who live by the Spirit should restore that person gently. But watch yourself, or you also may be tempted." (Galatians 6:1 NIV)

"Do not be misled: Bad company corrupts good character." (1 Corinthians 15:33 NIV)

3) THE WORLD: "Do not love the world or the things in the world. If anyone loves the world, the love of the Father is not in him. For all that is in the world—the desires of the flesh and the desires of the eyes and pride of life—is not from the Father but is from the world. And the world is passing away along with its desires, but whoever does the will of God abides forever." (1 John 1:15-17 ESV)

4) SATAN: "Be sober-minded; be watchful. Your adversary the devil prowls around like a roaring lion, seeking someone to devour. Resist him, firm in your faith, knowing that the same kinds of suffering are being experienced by your brotherhood throughout the world." (1 Peter 5:8-9 ESV)

In watchful prayer we remind ourselves where temptations might call out to us. We tell Our Father, and we confirm to ourselves, that we desire to stay on the path of life that leads upward toward eternal life, asking for wisdom from His Word to keep us from going down into the darkness of sin and eternal death (Proverbs 15:24).

Always available to encourage, Our Father's inspired words tell us, "I have taught you the way of wisdom; I have led you in right paths (Proverbs 4:11 NKJV). I will turn the darkness into light and the rough places into level ground. These are the things I do" (Isaiah 42:16 ESV).

As Jesus our Shepherd leads us, we will come to places where the road of righteousness crosses a super highway that passes through a wide gate—the route we did not choose. With Jesus we are traveling on a narrow road because we have already responded to his words:

> "Enter by the narrow gate. For the gate is wide and the way is easy that leads to destruction, and those who enter by it are many. For the gate is narrow and the way is hard that leads to life, and those who find it are few" (Matthew 7:13-14 ESV).

We made our decision to go through the narrow gate and to stay on the way of wisdom.

If not careful to remember that we chose the narrow gate that leads to life, the confusion of a moment may cause us to make a potentially disastrous wrong turn. As we watch the busy throngs traveling on the wide road, where they are going and what they are doing may look interesting. So much energy and excitement. We may take our eyes off Jesus. Someone in the crowd calls to us and we change lanes moving even further away from our chosen narrow way. Soon we pick up speed and travel with the traffic on the broad super highway . . . and we sin.

The temptation to travel for a while along a wider, faster route will eventually lead us into the congestion of sin. One day we just might find ourselves in a traffic jam of consequences from wrong choices and unwise decisions. When we need assistance to free us and get us moving once again on the right road and in the right direction, we may always call out to God, saying,

"Where am I? How did I get here? How do I get out of this? 'I have strayed like a lost sheep. Seek your servant for I have not forgotten your commands'" (Psalm 119:176 NIV).

Jesus, our Shepherd, is also the Highway Patrolman we need for times like these. He hears our pleas for help and searches for us. Jesus and Our Father in heaven are not willing that any should be lost (Matthew 18:12-14). When we have weakened in the face of temptation and have taken a wrong turn which leads us into sin, Jesus will find us and invite us back onto the path of life that leads us upward because He knows how to rescue sincere people from trials (2 Peter 2:9).

Whenever temptation confuses us and lures us onto the road of sin, Our Father will search for us and call us back to Himself. If His corrections are received in the spirit of love in which they are given, Our Shepherd will joyfully put us on His shoulders and return us to the path that leads to our heavenly home. We will rejoice together as we travel once again in the right direction. And, there will be great joy and rejoicing in heaven (Luke 15:7).

Every temptation comes with a decision, either to sin or to fully rely upon God. So often there is within us a self-sufficiency that says, "I don't want to bother God for help." This is a proud and dangerous thought! We need to pray. We must pray because even though our spirit is willing to follow Our Father's road map, our flesh is weak. Over the years when our sin has humbled us time and time again and we have felt ourselves "under great pressure, far beyond our ability to endure, so that we despair even of life" we begin to understand that the circumstances and events in our lives happen so "that we might not rely on ourselves but on God" (2 Corinthians 1:8-9 NIV).

Even though there are innumerable trials and temptations along the path that leads upward, we can rejoice because our faith is refined and proven genuine with each victory over sin (1 Peter 1:6-7).

As the journey with Jesus continues, if we do become careless and fail to watch and pray, our hearts may harden so that we make little effort to resist sin. When we become inattentive, neglecting prayer, the signposts warning of danger often are ignored as if we think we are above God's law.

→ "Stern discipline awaits the one who leaves the path; he who hates correction will die." (Proverbs 15:10 NIV)

→ "See to it, brothers and sisters, that none of you has a sinful, unbelieving heart that turns away from the living God. But encourage one another daily... so that none of you may be hardened by sin's deceitfulness." (Hebrews 3:12-13 NIV)

→ "Today, if you hear his voice, do not harden your hearts...." (Hebrews 3:7-8 ESV)

→ "... the Lord disciplines the one he loves." (Hebrews 12:6 ESV)

Our Father disciplines us. He allows stress and problems to engulf us. But He always provides a way out just as He has promised. Although He brings sorrow, He also has mercy and great love. He does not like to punish people or make them sad (Lamentations 3:31-33 NCV).

Our Father desires that sin and temptation not be taken lightly. Our attitude should be the same as that of Jesus who struggled and prayed when tempted, but did not sin. Jesus never mocked His Father by insulting the love they shared with a careless, detached attitude toward temptation. Our prayer must express our desire to be a person of "understanding who keeps a straight course" (Proverbs 15:21 NIV).

We resolve and confirm to Our Father that we will honor Him with our body (1 Corinthians 6:20). We will flee from the love of money and evil desires (1 Timothy 6:10, 2 Timothy 2:22). Our prayers reaffirm our desire to pursue righteousness, faith, love, peace and a pure heart (2 Timothy 2:22). We tell Him that our desire is to put to death whatever belongs to our earthly nature: sexual immorality, impurity, lust, evil desires and the idolatry of greed (Colossians 3:5).

In prayer we request strength and resolve so that we might stop anger and rage, stop purposely doing or saying things that hurt other people, stop filthy language and stop telling lies (Colossians 3:7-9).

With conviction we daily set our hearts and minds on things above, not on things that are on the earth (Colossians 3:1-2). We determine to persevere so that whatever we do, whether in word or deed, we do it all in the name of the Lord Jesus, giving thanks to God Our Father through Him (Colossians 3:17).

Continual pleasure in His company will be experienced as we travel the narrow road that leads heavenward, facing all outside pressures and temptations together.

Each time we are tempted we must remind ourselves that Jesus, our constant companion, faced every temptation that will ever cross our path. He suffered when tempted. We will suffer! He sympathizes and offers His help! He overcame! In His strength, we may overcome also! We will have the victory to overcome by the power of Jesus because He Himself overcame (1 John 5:4-5)!

With each new temptation, we must remember past temptations that were overcome because our strength was drawn from Him. Remembering the help we received in the past, fortifies us for the present. Our gratitude for what Jesus continually does for us expresses itself in prayer as we speak to Our Father,

> "When I thought, 'My foot slips,' your steadfast love, O LORD, held me up. When the cares of my heart are many, your consolations cheer my soul." (Psalm 94:18-19 ESV)

In our House of Prayer while in the pleasure of His company, we thank Him for His wonderful promises. And, we claim them as our own!

> "He Himself has said, 'I will never desert you, nor will I ever forsake you." (Hebrews 13:5b NASB)

> "Remember, God is the One who makes you and us strong in Christ." (2 Corinthians 1:21 NCV)

We rejoice in Our Father's promises that He is always with us. We are never alone! When we are tempted, He will make us strong enough not to give in to sin.

Even though we know with certainty that we are never alone, we know that 'the tempter' (Matthew 4:3, 1 Thessalonians 3:5) called 'the devil' is roaming like a lion. Looking for opportunity. Waiting for weakness. In the face of the ever-present danger of falling prey to the devil we entrust ourselves to Our Father, knowing that He has promised He will deliver us. Prayerfully we set our hope on the promise that He will deliver us again ... and again ... and again (2 Corinthians 1:10).

And so, we put our trust in Jesus who taught us to pray . . .

Chapter 12

"Deliver Us from the Evil One"

Matthew 6:13

The pleasure of fighting the good fight together

> "Submit yourselves, then, to God.
> Resist the devil, and he will flee from you.
> Come near to God and he
> will come near to you."
>
> James 4:7-8 NIV

Pray to Our Father in heaven. Listen for His wisdom. Hear with spiritual ears. See through spiritual eyes. Submit to Him. Be eager to obey His perfect will. Come near to Him. He will come near to us just as He has promised. He is as near as the breath within us, because His Spirit is in us. Our Father is not somewhere off beyond the clouds in a faraway place. His spirit surrounds us because when we are in Him, we are clothed in Jesus (Galatians 3:27). And, His spirit lives within us (John 14:17, Romans 8:9-11). We have only to take in a deep breath of air to experience in the physical, the likeness of the spiritual nearness of God.

In this life we know that many problems and temptations will continually attack us; therefore, we earnestly pray for deliverance. As we pray and verbalize all apprehension about our present experiences and our future temptations, the peace of God which goes beyond all understanding settles our nerves and calms our fears. His peace guards our hearts and minds in Christ Jesus (Philippians 4:7). Each one of us in Christ may have confidence in the face of any temptation, problem, illness, suffering, and even death because of Our Father's assurance that even though we walk through the valley of the shadow of death, we will fear no evil because Jesus is with us. He will always be there to comfort us (Psalm 23:4).

Each one of us is comforted and gives praise to Him, affirming, "You are my Shepherd. You are the Shepherd King who sits on the throne of my heart. You are the One whose voice I hear and whose will I desire to do. You are the one who sought me when I was lost and held me close to your heart (Matthew 18:12-13; Isaiah 40:11). You are the One who provides all I need for my daily life. You feed my soul with your spirit-breathed words. You are the one who leads me away from temptation. So, 'why should I fear when evil days come?' (Psalm 49:5 NIV)."

But we do have fears. And, when we do, we must bring our fears to God. We come near to Our Father in prayer. We submit ourselves to Him, praying to always resist the devil, trusting that the evil one will leave quickly (James 4:7-8). However, because we know there is constant danger, we plead in prayer,

"Deliver us from the evil one!"

We pray for God's help! We cannot fight in our own power. We are too weak. And if we think that we are strong, we need to be careful that we don't fall (1 Corinthians 10:12). Pride and arrogance, which God hates (Proverbs 8:13)—thinking we are strong enough to face the evil one on our own—may be the very weakness the devil will find to undermine our relationship with Our Father. We must always trust and rely on God and not on ourselves (2 Corinthians 1:9).

As we meditate upon Jesus' instructions to pray for deliverance from the evil one, once again it would be wise to examine ourselves. Maybe the reason we are not more successful in the face of temptation is because we have not asked for deliverance and thus have not received (James 4:3).

The evil one is known by many descriptive names:

- the ancient serpent called the devil, Satan, the deceiver of the whole world (Revelation 12:9 ESV)
- the great dragon (Revelation 12:9 ESV)
- the accuser of our brethren (Revelation 12:10b NKJV)
- Satan who fell from heaven like lightning (Luke 10:18 ESV)
- the father of lies (John 8:44 ESV)
- the spirit who is at work in those who are disobedient (Ephesians 2:2 ESV)

There was war in heaven when the evil one rose up against Almighty God. Pride filled his heart with desire to make himself like the Most High (Isaiah 14:14, Ezekiel 28:17). Our Father's loyal angels fought against Satan and against one third of the angels who aligned themselves with him; but the evil one "was not strong enough and he lost his place in heaven" (Revelation 12:8 NIV). He was hurled down to the earth and his angels with him, falling from heaven like lightning (Luke 10:18). From that time to this Satan has been trying and will continue to try to lead the whole world astray (Revelation 12:9).

Cast down into the realm of human kind, Satan roams like a lion (1 Peter 5:8) looking for sin and weakness in those who follow Jesus. He examines our actions, words, and motives. He accuses us day and night (Revelation 12:10b) and would lead us into the same condemnation as himself if it were not for Jesus who is "able to save forever those who draw near to God through Him, since He always lives to make intercession for them" (Hebrews 7:25 NASB).

Satan is our prosecutor. Jesus is our lawyer who pleads for us at the mercy seat of God. If the devil, who is truly well-named 'the evil one,' could destroy our eternal relationship with Our Father, he would do so. He is angry. In fact, he is filled with fury because "he knows that his time is short" (Revelation 12:12 NIV). So he growls and roams, shouts and accuses, hides and waits, looking for ways to destroy. There does not have to be an eternal bite to Satan's words because Jesus is absolutely and always able to save completely and forever those of us who come to him (Hebrews 7:25).

The evil one's anger and resolve to destroy everything Our Father has made beautiful knows no bounds as he sees his final day approaching—the last day when he will no longer be able to deceive and murder the souls of those who might have listened to and obeyed God. Satan's last day will come. He knows it will be soon.

Our Heavenly Father encourages us to focus on His Son's victory even though Satan's terrorism still surrounds us. We are assured that the war has already been won!

God assures us that "Our Savior, Christ Jesus... has destroyed death and has brought life and immortality to light through the gospel" (2 Timothy 1:10 NIV). Eternal life is already ours! The wonderful pleasure of His company forever! Reflect often on what Jesus has done and continues to do for us:

> "Since the children have flesh and blood, he too shared in their humanity so that by his death he might break the power of him who holds the power of death—that is, the devil—and free those who all their lives were held in slavery by their fear of death." (Hebrews 2:14-15 NIV)

Jesus became like one of us so He could fight for our freedom from God's law that says if we sin, we must die an eternal death (Romans 6:23), separated from God and condemned to the judgment given the evil one and his angels. Jesus was victorious over the evil one so that now those who look to the cross may receive the gift of God which is eternal life in Christ Jesus our Lord (Romans 6:23).

Jesus has won the war with Satan and the angels who turned against God. The victory already belongs to Jesus. We share in His victory as we share in all the blessings of being among the saved. However, even though the war has been won, not all the terrorists have been routed out. They hide. They disguise themselves. They pretend to be good when underneath they are evil. They hide in darkness. They continue their sneak attacks.

They entice us into danger. The evil one and his rebels continue to lurk in the shadows, plotting subversive action to surprise us with unexpected explosions of evil, attempting to massacre our faith and the faith of as many others as possible.

We must keep our focus and remember: The victory has already been won, even though skirmishes and battles continue! The victory is ours now!

We raise our prayerful voices in thanksgiving because Our Father always leads us in triumphal procession in Christ (2 Corinthians 2:14). As we follow Jesus on the path that leads upward, we are in the company of many others. Together we travel on the narrow road that leads to eternal life. We travel and shout praises of thanksgiving to God because He gives us the victory through our Lord Jesus Christ (1 Corinthians 15:57).

Our voices are raised in victory shouts as Our Father cheers us on through His inspired words, assuring us, "For everyone who has been born of God overcomes the world. And this is the victory that has overcome the world—our faith" (1 John 5:4 ESV). Our faith in the victory at the cross and our ongoing obedient faith in our Victorious Jesus will bring us safely through our time of occupation on this earth where, by faith, we must continually "fight the good fight of faith" (1 Timothy 6:12 NKJV).

We fight against all sources of temptation, whether from the evil one, from ourselves, from the world, or from unbelievers. Knowing the evil one has hidden 'sleeper cells', we must always be careful to choose our companions wisely. We must heed the warning not to listen to the counsel of the wicked, nor to spend time with those who prefer to leave their sins unforgiven. We must stay away from those who mock and scoff at the counsel of God (Psalms 1:1), fully accepting the truth that bad company corrupts good character (1 Corinthians 15:33 NIV). We must stay close to Jesus as we travel on the road that leads home to heaven, careful not to stray into the company of terrorists in disguise who would try to ambush us.

Yes, we fight the good fight of faith! It's a 'good' fight because we have already won the war! We can win all confrontations along the way because we hang on firmly to the reality of eternal life which is promised to us. And we hang on firmly to our ongoing confession that Jesus is the Son of God and our Savior (1 Timothy 6:12).

From the cross until the last day when Jesus comes to put the final end to the evil one and his followers, unseen spiritual forces will terrorize God's people. Our Father provides us with His wisdom for every battle. His 'Field Manual' details survival skills available to all who search His words for instruction. His desire is that as we read and pray, we cast all our anxiety, concern, fear, and worry on Him because He cares for us (1 Peter 5:8).

As we read His directives (1 Peter 5:8-9), Our Father warns:

- ➢ Be sober! Take this seriously!
- ➢ Be vigilant and alert! Watch out!
- ➢ Resist the devil! Refuse to give in!
- ➢ Stand firm in your faith!

We read and understand the warning is also for our brothers and sisters in Christ throughout the world who are undergoing these same kinds of temptations and sufferings (1 Peter 5:9).

Continuing to pour over Our Father's 'Field Manual' we understand that we are to pray for one another—family, friends, brothers and sisters in Christ. When we, or they, are under great pressure, far beyond the ability to endure, so that we, or they, despair even of life, we remember that these things happen so that we might not rely on ourselves but on God. We are to help each other by our prayers. We and they are strengthened when we pray for each other. Our brothers and sisters around the world are strengthened in their sufferings through our empathetic compassion as we pray for them (2 Corinthians 1:3-11).

Our Father's inspired words comfort us affirming in response to our prayer, "Deliver us from the evil one,"

> "He <u>has delivered</u> us...
> and he <u>will deliver</u> us....
> He <u>will deliver us again</u>...."
> (2 Corinthians 1:10 ESV underlined emphasis by author)

Our deliverance is like the very nature of God's being as described in His name, IAM THAT I AM. He transcends time because He lives in eternity. His name reveals that He has always been present, He is present now, and He will always be present in the future. Because of this, I have been delivered in the past. I am delivered even now. And, I will be delivered in the future. Our Father is always near to deliver us from the danger of the evil one as we pray for His protection and look for His way of escape.

Wanting us to continue to remain strong in the darkness of any temptation and in the obscured vision of every disappointment, Our Father gives us night vision glasses. He gives us eyes to look into the spiritual realm where by faith we search through a greenish haze and see the reality of our conflicts. Through Our Father's words we see our enemy and realize that "our struggle is not against flesh and blood, but against the rulers, against the authorities, against the powers of this dark world and against the spiritual forces of evil in the heavenly realms" (Ephesians 6:12 NIV).

Sometimes we would prefer to stay in hiding rather than fight against the attacks of the evil one and his army. Fear can paralyze us into cowardice where we would seek to dress ourselves in camouflage material so we look more like the world. We hope the evil one will not take notice of us. Life becomes too dangerous, we may think, so we try to escape any way we can. We try to hide deep in the trenches of denial, isolation, work, or busy-ness. Some try to escape into alcohol or drugs. Or maybe we try to escape by spending hours in front of the television. Sometimes we escape into music played so loud we don't have to think. Anything! so we don't have to confront our problems and temptations in open conflict.

We dare not deceive ourselves into thinking that we are safe because we run and hide. The fact is, if we desert our fellow believers and those who pray for us, we align ourselves with "the cowardly" who await the same punishment as "the unbelieving, the vile, the murderers, the sexually immoral, those who practice magic arts, the idolaters and all liars" (Revelation 21:8 NIV).

151

Jesus, who is the same yesterday, today, and forever (Hebrews 13:8), is the One who spoke through the prophet Moses when God's people were fearful of the battle ahead of them. These same words of hope (Deuteronomy 20:3-4 NIV) transcend time to become ours as we face our battles:

> ➢ "Today you are going into battle against your enemies.
> ➢ Do not be fainthearted or afraid;
> ➢ Do not be terrified or give way to panic before them.
> ➢ For the LORD your God is the one who goes with you to fight for you against your enemies to give you victory."

Although we may try to hide the nakedness of our fear, God through His inspired words calls us out of our cowardice. We are commanded, "Be strong in the Lord and in his great power" (Ephesians 6:10 NCV). "Put aside the deeds of darkness and put on the armor of light... clothe yourselves with the Lord Jesus Christ" (Romans 13:12, 14 NIV).

The armor of light is Jesus Christ Himself! Clothed with His light, the darkness that surrounds us does not seem so dark. Seeing the battle through His eyes and fighting in His strength, gives us courage for today and for whatever may wait in hiding for our future.

Having prayed to Our Father for daily spiritual bread and then nourishing ourselves with His words, we are strengthened for conflicts because now the Word of God lives in us (1 John 2:13). Because of the knowledge which comes from Our Father, Our Commander in Chief, we are instructed to dress in our heavenly issued battle gear. Our uniform is not camouflage material. Our armor is spiritual, even though likened to the armor of the

Roman soldiers who were visible everywhere during the time of Jesus and the early church.

By faith and in prayer, we prepare ourselves daily for deliverance from the evil one. We prepare ourselves by following His instructions (Ephesians 6:11, 13 NIV):

> ➢ "Put on the full armor of God.
> ➢ Take your stand against the devil's schemes.
> ➢ Stand your ground.
> ➢ After you have done everything, stand!"

The armor we are to wear guarantees that we will stand and not fall. Our Savior does not want us to "fall away" (Hebrews 6:6 NKJV). He does not want us to "fall into temptation" (Matthew 26:41 NIV). He does not want us to "fall into sin" (1 Corinthians 8:13 NIV). He does not want us to "fall short of the glory of God" (Romans 3:23 ESV).

Our Heavenly Commander wants us to . . .

> ➢ Be on our guard!
> ➢ Stand firm in the faith!
> ➢ Be courageous!
> ➢ Be strong!
>
> 1 Corinthians 16:13 NIV

Our Father wants us to stand against the devil's schemes and after we have done everything, to stand! He promises if we do the things He requests, we will never fall. He promises we will be given a wonderful welcome into the eternal kingdom of our Lord and Savior Jesus Christ (2 Peter 1:10-11).

We pray and tell Our Father, "Yes, I want to stand firm! I want to be courageous! I want to be strong!" Each individual must suit up in their own personally-fitted armor of light. Each person must be certain to always be ready to take their stand against the devil's schemes, deceitful tricks, and lies. Each one must look into the 'Field Manual' and read:

- "Therefore take up the whole armor of God that you may be able to withstand in the evil day, and having done all, to stand firm.
- Stand therefore, having fastened on the belt of truth,
- and having put on the breastplate of righteousness,
- and as shoes for your feet, having put on the readiness given by the gospel of peace.
- In all circumstances take up the shield of faith, with which you can extinguish all the flaming darts of the evil one;
- and take the helmet of salvation,
- and the sword of the Spirit, which is the word of God, praying at all times in the Spirit…."
  (Ephesians 6:13-18 ESV underline emphasis by author)

"Deliver us from the evil one," we pray daily, pausing to visualize dressing ourselves in each part of the armor of light. Each day we clothe ourselves anew in Jesus as we review our eternal protection. Suiting up properly confirms to Him that we believe He exists and that He will reward those of us who diligently seek Him (Hebrews 11:6).

Once again, the 'we' must become 'I'. Praying and preparing myself for each day, I fasten the belt of truth around my waist. My heavenly issued belt must be fastened securely because it holds the sheath for my sword of the Spirit which is the Word—all the words—of God. Resolving that nothing false will attach itself to me, I promise Our Father that I will continue to follow Jesus' teachings like a true disciple, knowing that His truth will protect my soul (John 8:31-32). As I cinch the belt into place, my prayer is that I will always not only hear His words but do them (Luke 11:28)!

Standing firm in the grace and peace I have with God through Jesus (Romans 5:1-2), I put on my breastplate of righteousness (Ephesians 6:14), the breastplate that is also called "faith and love" (1 Thessalonians 5:8). Fastened securely over my chest, it protects every breath I breathe and every beat of my heart. As I see righteousness covering my heart—the spiritual representation of my emotions, my love and my faithfulness—I lift my voice in praise to Our Father because He made Jesus who had no sin to be sin for me so that in Him I might share in His perfect, sinless nature and become righteous (2 Corinthians 5:21). His protective righteousness comes through faith and is available to all of us who believe (Romans 3:22). Jesus is our righteousness. He covers our sins with His righteousness and protects us in the same way that the breastplate protected the heart of a well-dressed soldier.

Having promised Our Father to continue to walk in the truth (3 John 1:3) and remain under the protection of the righteousness of Jesus, I put on the shoes that go with my armor of light. With these spiritual shoes on my feet I am ready to stand and live and move in Christ (Acts 17:28).

At first, when these spiritual shoes are new, they might not be as comfortable as we would like. But we chose them and we determine to wear them. Our shoes become more and more comfortable with use. Our shoes are ready to take us wherever God leads for the sake of the gospel. We must never go about spiritually barefoot. Our shoes must be worn daily so that we are ready! Always prepared for anyone who might ask us about our faith and hope in Jesus our Savior (1 Peter 3:15).

In all confrontations with temptations and with those people in this world who are "under the control of the evil one" (1 John 5:19 NIV), we are able to move quickly in our well-fitted shoes to flee sin according to God's battle plan or to stand firm with our feet of faith well-grounded in the knowledge of the death, burial and resurrection of Jesus. We continue to stand strong, holding onto the words of Jesus (2 Thessalonians 2:15).

And, we march in the steps of Jesus. We "keep in step with the Spirit" (Galatians 5:25 ESV). His cadence sounds off with each step: Love! Joy! Peace! Patience! Kindness! Goodness! Faithfulness! Gentleness! Self-control (Galatians 5:22-23)!

Wherever Our Father leads, we are prepared to overcome evil with good (Romans 12:21). Along life's journey we speak about our victories over the evil one. We share God's battle strategies with others so they may be victorious also! We recruit for the Lord's army and help new soldiers dress in the armor of Jesus. Everywhere we go we pray to hear Jesus say, "How beautiful are the feet of those who bring good news of good things (Romans 10:15 NASB)!"

As Our Father's victorious ranks marching to heaven grow larger, the soldiers in step with Jesus speak every language of the world. Together we rejoice that through faith we are all shielded by God's power (1 Peter 1:5).

Alert and watching for snipers along the way, Our Father commands us to take up the shield of faith! Take it up for protection from the flaming arrows of the evil one (Ephesians 6:16). Our Father promises to be our strength and shield (Psalm 28:7). In truth, each one of us must believe and trust, telling ourselves, "My shield is God Most High, who saves the upright in heart" (Psalm 7:10 NIV).

By faith we trust that God Most High is ready to deliver us from the evil one. The shield that we must carry for protection will surely deliver us from the evil one because the shield is not my faith which sometimes grows tired and weak. It is His faithfulness that shields me (Psalm 91:4)!

Our Father's shield of faith will protect us from any weapon that might be fired in our direction. We pray that "when they draw the bow, let their arrows fall short (Psalm 58:7 NIV)." Our Father's faithfulness shields us from any burning arrows that the evil one may draw into his bow and aim toward us. We will not fear the terror of night nor the arrow that flies by day (Psalm 91:5). We may be wounded from time to time, but no eternal harm will come to us from the flaming arrows of the evil one. Neither the devil nor any of his evil angels can burn away my faith with their flammable accusations, scorching temptations, or smoldering problems.

Our Father and His Son by the power of His Spirit will deliver us from the mouth of the dragon, called the devil and Satan, whose fury burns because he knows his time is short. God will rescue our souls from every evil attack, every evil deed, and every hurtful thing. He will bring us safely to our final, eternal, heavenly destination (2 Timothy 4:18).

Marching in step with the spirit, we respond immediately when the One who orders our steps, says, "Put on the hope of salvation as a helmet" (1 Thessalonians 5:8: Ephesians 6:17). Our Father is not fitting us as soldiers in His army in order to prepare us to suffer wrath—His or that of the evil one—but to have salvation through our Lord Jesus Christ (1 Thessalonians 5:9). Each one of us march saying, "I have been saved, I am saved, and I will be saved." This knowledge is like a helmet protecting the head—mind and thoughts—of each soldier in Christ. Each one who wears the armor of light may say, "Our Father shields my head in the day of battle" (Psalm 140:7 NIV). But as long as there is evil in this world, each one of us should be praying, "O Sovereign Lord, my strong deliverer... do not grant the wicked their desires, O Lord; do not let their plans succeed" (Psalm 140:7-8 NIV).

When our time comes to stand and fight, we "take the sword of the Spirit, which is the word of God. We pray in the Spirit at all times with all kinds of prayers, asking for everything we need. To do this we must always be ready and never give up" (Ephesians 6:17-18 NCV).

Our sword that has been resting in the sheath firmly attached to our belt of truth will be drawn and skillfully used in response to any attack because we have prepared our minds for action (1 Peter 1:13). We have studied the words of God, and we know how to wield His inspired words correctly.

In the face of evil, we raise our spiritual swords and lunge forward in prayer. We swing one way and then another. We pray, and we keep on praying. We speak the words of God to fend off the blows that would weaken us, cause us to sin, or wound our faith. We fight with all our mind, heart, and strength.

We encourage ourselves with the wisdom from God who says that His every word is flawless! Pure! True! Tested! (Proverbs 30:5). We are spiritually protected every time we draw our sword of the Spirit—the words He spoke to us which are spirit and life (John 6:63).

> "For though we walk in the flesh, we are not waging war according to the flesh. For the weapons of our warfare are not of the flesh but have divine power to destroy strongholds. We destroy arguments and every lofty opinion raised against the knowledge of God, and take every thought captive to obey Christ...."
> (2 Corinthians 10:3-5 ESV)

When evil times come upon us and we feel ourselves under attack, we recognize our inability to protect ourselves on our own. In our own power, we are weaker than the evil one. Be assured, however, there is hope! Jesus who is always with us has all authority in heaven and on earth (Matthew 28:18). Because of written testimony from eyewitnesses to Jesus' miracles, we can be assured that with authority and power He gives orders to evil spirits and they come out (Luke 4:36 NCV).

When I take a firm stand against sin or any kind of problem, Jesus stands with me. The One who gives orders to evil spirits can and will deliver me from any harm they might use against me. Jesus is in me and I am in Him. And, I know that the one who is in me is greater than the evil one who is in the world. Together, Jesus and I overcome them (1 John 4:4), and we will continue to overcome.

As we fight on against sin, Jesus protects us and keeps us safe. The evil one cannot harm us (1 John 5:18). The Lord is faithful, and He will strengthen and protect us from the evil one (2 Thessalonians 3:3).

Being one spirit with our brother Jesus and fighting together against evil influences and sin that would enter and destroy this relationship, our minds truly need to be in harmony with His. We must think as He thinks so we can face the enemy united in thought and will. Until we realize that our attitude toward the evil one must be the complete opposite of love, we may lose more skirmishes and battles than we win. And when we do win, we may come away more deeply wounded because our feelings toward our enemy were not strong enough to motivate us to resist as vehemently as Our Father would desire.

The word 'hate' is seldom spoken in polite circles. It is a word that has fallen almost into disuse because it has often been misused; however, we must firmly grasp the reality that God hates. In fact, Our Father commands those who love Him to hate evil! Not to rationalize evil! Not to attempt to put a tolerant spin on evil! Not to ignore evil! But to hate evil!

May each one of us prayerfully resolve to have the same intense mind set about evil as that of Our Deliverer:

- "Let those who love the Lord <u>hate evil</u>, for he guards the lives of his faithful ones and delivers them from the hand of the wicked." (Psalm 97:10 NIV)

- "To fear the LORD is to <u>hate evil</u>; I hate pride and arrogance, evil behavior and perverse speech." (Proverbs 8:13 NIV)

- "<u>Hate evil</u> and love good...." (Amos 5:15 ESV)

- "<u>Hate what is evil</u>; cling to what is good." (Romans 12:9 NIV)
  (Underlined emphasis by author)

When we feel as if we face death all day long (Psalm 44:22 NIV); and, in our battles of life rather than triumphant soldiers we feel like "sheep being led to the slaughter" (Romans 8:36 NIV), we must pray and continue to stand firm. Our Father will always renew our strength and our minds with His flawless words of truth.

When we are battle weary, the same sword that demolishes everything that sets itself up against God—the same sword which wields the words of God—encourages us to stand and keep standing. The Spirit's God-breathed words assure us that "in all these things we are more than conquerors through him who loved us" (Romans 8:37 ESV).

As we pray daily to be delivered from the evil one, spiritual adrenalin renews our strength as the question, "If God is for us, who shall be against us?" (Romans 8:31 ESV) rings in our ears. The answer shouts to us: No one! Nothing will be able to separate us from the love of God that is in Christ Jesus our Lord (Romans 8:39).

Whenever and wherever we are attacked, Our Father is there (Psalm 139:7)! The Son of God leads in battle those who follow in his footsteps (Matthew 28:20, 1 Peter 2:21)! He continually provides us with everything we need to live and serve Him (2 Peter 1:3). He provides everything we need to be victorious!

As Our Father's will becomes more deeply imbedded in our hearts and minds, we give a victory shout as we continue to pray "that we will be rescued from perverse and evil men; for not all have faith. But the Lord is faithful, and he will strengthen and protect us from the evil one" (2 Thessalonians 3:2 NASV).

All the gratitude and love we feel for Him because of His continual deliverance and protection fills our hearts to overflowing.

From deep within us we lift our voices in joyful praise, praying . . .

Chapter 13

_豕_

"For Yours is the Kingdom and the Power and the Glory Forever. Amen."
Matthew 6:13

Thanking Him for the pleasure of His company

> "For the Lord takes delight in his people
> He crowns the humble with salvation.
> Let the saints rejoice in this honor
> and sing for joy....
> May the praise of God be in their mouths
> and a double-edged sword in their hands....
> Praise the Lord!"
> Psalm 149:4-6, 9 NIV

Rejoice in the wonderful honor to hold in our hands the double-edged sword of faith—the very words of God that will judge the world (John 12:48)! Praise the Lord because we are soldiers in Our Father's army, fighting for the will of God to be done on earth as it is in heaven! Delight ourselves in Him as we humbly wear the helmet of

salvation that He has provided for our heads! Sing for joy as
we receive deliverance from the evil one and as we receive
victory over sin and death! Praise the Lord as our eternal,
spiritual relationship grows deeper day by day because we are
enjoying the pleasure of His company in meaningful prayer
and meditation upon His words. And, even better than our
own joy in His presence is the knowledge that Our Father
takes delight in us!

Yes, we thank Him for all He has done. We thank Him for what
He has done for each one of us on a very personal and intimate
level. Each one in Jesus truly finds a completeness of heart,
mind, body and soul as we delight ourselves in the Lord and
He gives us the desires of our hearts (Psalm 37:4). He gives us
daily what we need for body and soul. We have asked Him and
thanked Him for every blessing received.

The joy of our salvation grows more precious each time we are
forgiven. The more we confess to Our Father our desire to live
according to His will, the more His words begin to come from
our mouths in joyful praise. When joy because of our salvation
fills our hearts and minds, we cannot and must not keep silent.
Our increase of joy because of the hope we have will find ways
to express itself to others. Then, we will teach God's ways and
His plans to unbelievers and those who do wrong, and they will
be converted to Him (Psalm 51:12-13).

In joyful praise and prayer, we tell Our Father,

> "I will praise you, O Lord, among the nations;
> I will sing of you among the peoples,
> For great is your love, higher than the heavens;

your faithfulness reaches to the skies.
Be exalted, O God, above the heavens,
and let your glory be over all the earth!"
Psalm 108:3-5 NIV

Those of us who are among the "redeemed of the Lord
will say this: Oh, give thanks to the Lord, for He is good;
for His loving kindness is everlasting" (Psalm 107:1-2 NASB).
We will be joyful always. We will continue to pray and give
thanks in all circumstances because this is God's will for us
(1 Thessalonians 5:16-18).

With one heart and mouth, all those of us who follow the
Savior of the world will glorify the God and Father of our
Lord Jesus Christ (Romans 15:5-6). Together we will sing
hymns to His name (Romans 15:9). Together we will call on
His name and make known among the nations what He
has done, and at every opportunity we will exalt His name
(Isaiah 16:4).

After praying as Jesus taught His followers, let us join together
to pray these closing words of praise:

"For Yours is the Kingdom"

Our minds and hearts return again to the wonderful relationship
we have with our King whom we invite daily to remain upon
the throne of our hearts.

We continually praise Our Father because He "has freed us
from the power of darkness and brought us into the kingdom
of his dear Son" (Colossians 1:13 NCV). As long as time shall

last, we will praise Him because He will continue to rescue us from everything evil and will bring us safely into His heavenly kingdom (2 Timothy 4:18).

In our House of Prayer we thank God for inviting us into His kingdom. We praise Him, saying:

> "Now to the King eternal, immortal,
> invisible, the only God,
> be honor and glory for ever and ever.
> Amen."
>
> 1 Timothy 1:17 NASB

We thank Him for His eternal, glorious kingdom of heaven. We thank Him for inviting us to share everything in His kingdom. We thank Him that His kingdom has come upon us (Matthew 12:28) and that His kingdom is within us (Luke 17:21)! Even though in the kingdom of this world we hear about—or personally experience—tragedy, disease, injustice, oppression, starvation, abuse, and wars, we thank God because His kingdom is not of this world (John 18:36). We praise Him because He has bestowed upon us an eternal and higher citizenship which is in heaven (Philippians 3:20).

"For Yours is ... the Power"

We verbalize in praise and thanksgiving our sincere appreciation for His divine power. We thank Him for providing us with everything we need for life and godliness. We thank Our Father for the knowledge of Jesus revealed through His Word to everyone He calls by His Spirit of glory and goodness (2 Peter 1:3)!

We have prayed about our weaknesses and have meditated on His powerful words until we found our strength in Him. And we will continue to pray in the pleasure of His company, trusting His promise that we can do everything through Him who gives us the strength we need for every life experience (Philippians 4:13). We rejoice because "He gives strength to those who are tired and more power to those who are weak. The people who trust the Lord will become strong again" (Isaiah 40:29, 31 NCV).

As we have meditated upon the encouragement that for those who love God all things work together for good (Romans 8:28), we may wonder how that can possibly happen when there are so many disappointments in our lives. While we wait to see what good He will work out, we praise Him! When we face anything that brings anxiety, rather than allowing our concern to turn into "fretting which only causes harm" (Psalm 37:7-8 NKJV), we praise Him for what He has done in the past, for what He is doing now, and for what He will do in the future!

When the uncertainty of the time and circumstances of our physical death enters our thoughts, we will praise Him for His power in which we will share. We will lay our fears at the feet of our King and take from Him the knowledge that comes from Our Father, believing and praising because . . .

> "By his power God raised the Lord from the dead,
> and he will raise us also."
> 1 Corinthians 6:14 NIV

In prayer we have put on the armor of light which is Jesus Himself, and we rejoice once again that through faith we are "shielded by God's power" (1 Peter 1:15 NIV). No matter what the present or the future holds Our Father's power will protect our eternal relationship in Jesus Christ.

As we daily approach the throne of Our Father and Jesus our King, we will sing of His strength and power and love (Psalm 59:16). Our voices will join with every creature in heaven and on earth singing, "To the One who sits on the throne and to the Lamb be praise and honor and glory and power forever and ever" (Revelation 5:13 NCV). Our hearts will rejoice in His presence! We will honor Him with all of our hearts, minds, and spirits!

"For Yours is ... the Glory"

Having praised Him in prayer because of His kingdom and power, we pause to meditate upon His glory. God's glory is the radiance of His perfect character. Our Father's character is absolute perfection. Our Savior Jesus Christ has a perfect character. "The Son is the radiance of God's glory and the exact representation of his being" (Hebrews 1:3 NIV).

Even those who sought to find fault with Jesus recognized His character as a man. They said, "We know you are a man of integrity. You aren't swayed by men, because you pay no attention to who they are; but you teach the way of God in accordance with the truth" (Mark 12:14 NIV). Those of us who desire to become more and more like Jesus will set His character as our goal.

Jesus was an honest man, a man of character who "committed no sin and no deceit was found in his mouth. When they hurled their insults at him, he did not retaliate; when he suffered, he made no threats. Instead, he entrusted himself to him who judges justly" (1 Peter 2:22-23 NIV). Just as Jesus understood, so must we, that "if you are insulted because of the name of Christ, you are blessed, for the Spirit of glory and of God rests on you" (1 Peter 4:14 ESV).

Jesus trusted His Father because the desire of Jesus' heart was to do His Father's will and to teach only what His Father instructed. In honesty and integrity of character Jesus did not teach His own opinions or soften His words to make them more palatable to the traditions and religious interpretations of His times. As people of character who desire to bring glory to God in all things, neither should we. The words of Jesus must become our words in order to bring glory to Our Father. He said, "My teaching is not mine, but his who sent me. If anyone's will is to do God's will, he will know whether the teaching is from God or whether I am speaking on my own authority. The one who speaks on his own authority seeks his own glory; but the one who seeks the glory of him who sent him is true, and in him there is no falsehood" (John 7:16-18 ESV).

As we continue in an attitude of prayer and meditation, focusing on God's glory, we rejoice in God who is light—the kind of light in which there is no darkness at all (1 John 1:5). We remember our sincere prayer request, "Lead us not into temptation." We remember that the desire of our hearts is not to walk in darkness, but to walk in the light, as Jesus is in the light, so that we might have eternal fellowship with one another (1 John 1:6-7). We desire to enjoy now and into eternity fellowship with our family in Christ and fellowship with Our Father, His Son, and the Holy Spirit (1 John 1:3; 2 Corinthians 13:14).

We bring glory to His name when we speak about the wonderful, miraculous things He has accomplished. We bring Him great honor when we speak to others about His glorious, powerful deeds. We speak about the wonder and power of His creation. We tell others about the glory of God that raised Jesus from the dead. We speak about our own immersion into death in order that, just as Christ was raised from the dead by the glory of the Father, we also were raised to walk in newness of life (Romans 6:4-5 ESV). We share with others, to the glory of God, how we were united with Him in a death like his; and we shall certainly also be united with him in a resurrection like his. We speak about the glory of His resurrection and our own promised glory.

We speak about the splendor of heaven and the wonders of our eternal home. In doing so, we bring glory to His name. We bring glory that reaches the ears and hearts of people here on earth and glory that is heard by angels in heaven.

Everyone in Jesus participates in His glory as we walk in His light. We see and hear and praise because of the pure light that comes from God, who said, "Let light shine out of darkness" (2 Corinthians 4:6 ESV). And we continue praising because He is "the same God who made his light shine in our hearts by letting us know the glory of God that is in the face of Christ" (2 Corinthians 4:6 NCV).

Our Father gives us His glorious light because of Jesus. Just as Jesus reflected Our Father's glory, we reflect His glory. All of us in Christ will reflect our Lord's glory. His glory will change us, transforming us into His likeness from one degree of glory to another (2 Corinthians 3:18). Glory is reflected back to Our Father as our character is perfected through Jesus.

Jesus said to Our Father, "I have glorified You on the earth. I have finished the work which You have given Me to do"

(John 17:4 NKJV). The work of Jesus was to fulfill all that was required to open the doors of heaven for all who were denied entrance because they were spiritually dead because of sin. He triumphed over sin and death. At the end of our lives on earth may we also be able to say that we have brought Our Father glory because we have done all He has asked us to do, standing firm by faith and trusting in Jesus in all things.

The One who leads us to heaven and whose glory we reflect says, "This is to my Father's glory, that you bear much fruit, and so prove to be my disciples" (John 15:8 ESV).

Our Father is always encouraging, comforting and urging each one of us to "live lives worthy of God because He is calling us heavenward into his kingdom and glory" (1 Thessalonians 2:12 NIV). Not only is He encouraging us through the glory and power of Jesus by equipping us with everything good for doing his will so that He may work in us what is pleasing to Him (Hebrews 13:21), but He is promising that "to those who by persistence in doing good seek glory, honor and immortality, he will give eternal life" (Romans 2:7 NIV).

Our Father's promises are trustworthy. May they fill our hearts with joy and our minds with determination so that when we speak, we speak only the words of God. When we serve, we serve with the strength God provides. May we speak and do so that "in all things God may be praised through Jesus Christ. To him be the glory and the power for ever and ever. Amen" (1 Peter 4:11 NIV).

May we always pray for strength and rely upon His power so that whether we eat or drink or whatever we do, we do it all for the glory of God (1 Corinthians 10:31). May we give everything we have to the glory of God. May we give ourselves, our time, our prayers, our priorities, our energy, our money, and our praise to Him. In those reflective, humble moments in the pleasure of Our Father's company, may our honest words be, "I glory in Christ Jesus in my service to God" (Romans 15:17 NIV).

May the glory we bring Our Father become ever brighter as we seek to serve Him in His kingdom on earth as we are served by Him in the kingdom of heaven. May we bring Him joy and delight. May we grow in the grace and knowledge of our Lord and Savior Jesus Christ (2 Peter 3:18) so that our loving service may become more and more effective.

May the desires of our hearts be the answer to the prayer of the apostle Paul:

> "This is my prayer for you: that your love will grow more and more; that you will have knowledge and understanding with your love; that you will see the difference between good and bad and will choose the good; that you will be pure and without wrong for the coming of Christ; that you will be filled with the good things produced in your life by Christ to bring glory and praise to God." (Philippians 1:9-11 NCV)

Our prayers of praise continually thank God for His invitation to share in His glory! Even though every one of us has sinned and fallen short of the glory of God (Romans 3:23), Our Father invites us to share in His glory. By faith we see Jesus bringing many to glory (Hebrews 2:10) and we rejoice because in Jesus we are among them.

We are God's children and heirs of eternal life, "heirs with Christ, provided we suffer with him in order that we may also be glorified with him" (Romans 8:17 ESV). We must "consider that the sufferings of this present time are not worth comparing with the glory that is to be revealed to us" (Romans 8:18 ESV).

As we praise Our Father, rejoicing in the glory of His grace, His promise is ours:

> "The God of all grace, who called you to His
> eternal glory in Christ, after you have suffered
> a little while, will himself restore you and make
> you strong, firm and steadfast. To Him be the
> power forever. Amen." (1 Peter 5:10 NIV)

"Yours . . . Forever!"

'Forever' is the final word of the final phrase as recorded in Scripture for the prayer that Jesus taught His followers. The will of God on earth as it is in heaven is that we praise Him forever! Eternally! It is His will that "at the name of Jesus every knee should bow, in heaven and on earth and under the earth, and every tongue confess that Jesus Christ is Lord, to the glory of God the Father" (Philippians 2:10-11 ESV).

Our praises on earth reach into eternity as we rejoice, "Blessed be his glorious name forever; may the whole earth be filled with his glory. Amen and Amen" (Psalm 72:19 ESV).

And as we come to the throne of Our Father in prayer—His throne that will last for ever and ever (Hebrews 1:8)—with spiritual ears we hear eternal praises: "To him who sits on the throne and to the Lamb be praise and honor and glory and power, forever and ever" (Revelation 5:13 NIV)!

In the final days of His life upon the earth, Jesus took His apostles aside and told them, "You have sorrow now, but I will see you again, and your hearts will rejoice, and no one will take your joy from you" (John 16:22 ESV).

Jesus explained that He was going away and that He would no longer be with them in the same way as the previous three and a half years. There would be many things His disciples and all those who would come after them would need and many requests that must be made. Even before His disciples fully understood what was to happen and before they could ask the question about how to communicate their requests after He was gone from their physical presence, He spoke the words of promise which the Spirit would later bring to their minds:

> "Truly, truly, I say to you, whatever you ask of the Father <u>in my name</u>, he will give it to you. Until now you have asked nothing in my name. Ask, and you will receive, that your joy may be full."
> (John 16:23-24 ESV underlined emphasis by author)

From the time the Son returned to His Father until now, when we pray, we ask,

"In the name of Jesus!"

When we ask for conviction and courage to do His will, we close our prayer, saying, "In the name of Jesus!" When we ask for better discipline to keep Him on the throne of our hearts, we finish our prayer saying, "In Jesus' name!" With every request for physical and spiritual needs, as we pray for ourselves and for others, we end our requests, "In the name of Jesus we pray!" When the evil one attacks with temptations, illnesses, and disappointments, and we struggle for victory, we pray, "In the power of Jesus' name!"

Jesus intercedes for us, presenting every request to Our Father. As we ask according to His will, Jesus has promised to do whatever we ask so that He may bring glory to the Father, saying that if we ask for anything in His name, He will do it (John 14:13). May we give glory to Our Father and to Jesus Our Intercessor knowing that our requests are heard and carefully considered at the heavenly throne.

We do all and pray all things in the name of Jesus Christ who is far above all rule and authority and power and dominion, and "above every name that is named, not only in this age but also in the one to come" (Ephesians 1:21 ESV). We pray in the name of Jesus because He "lives forever… and is able to save completely those who come to God through him, because he always lives to intercede for us" (Hebrews 7:24-25 NIV).

It is in His name that the nations put their hope (Matthew 12:21 NIV). It is in His name that each follower places their trust when praying. It is in His name that our salvation is found. "Our salvation is found in no one else, for there is no other name under heaven given to men by which we must be saved" (Acts 4:12 NIV).

When we pray, asking in His name, and when we have received according to His will, our joy is complete! Our delight in the pleasure of His company is beyond description. With the multitudes in heaven we shout, "Hallelujah! Salvation and glory and power belong to our God" (Revelation 19:1 ESV).

Amen!

"These are the words of the Amen,
the faithful and true witness,
the ruler of God's creation."
Revelation 3:14 NIV

Jesus is called "Amen," the final word and authority in everything in all creation.

"Amen!" we say as we close our prayer. And in the saying of this word we speak the very name of Jesus.

"Amen!" we say again and again as we hear and read every faithful and true word from Our Father through the mouth of His Son Jesus and through the inspiration of His Holy Spirit.

"Amen!" we pray telling Our Father that we desire to be in harmony with His will in all things.

Yes, Father, "Amen! may the Lord do so" (Jeremiah 28:6 NASB)!

Yes, Father, what you say is true! Yes, Father, your words and your promises are trustworthy!

Sometimes as we say "Amen," the closing word of our prayer, we may desire to linger awhile longer in His presence. What joy can be ours to read again a few of the many prayers that were said for us so very long ago. As we meditate upon the words, we linger intimately in the pleasure of Our Father's company.

Read and let your heart and mind listen to the words that were prayed for us.

Jesus prayed for us:

> "I pray also for those who will believe in me through their (the apostles') message, that all of them may be one, Father, just as you are in me and I am in you. May they also be in us so that the world may believe that you have sent me. I have given them the glory that you gave me, that they may be one as we are one: I in them and you in me. May they be brought to complete unity to let the world know that you sent me and have loved them even as you have loved me. Father, I want those you have given me to be with me where I am, and to see my glory, the glory you have given me because you loved me before the creation of the world!"
> (John 17:20-24 NIV)

Paul prayed for us:

> "For this reason I bow my knees before the Father, from whom every family in heaven and on earth is named, that according to the riches of his glory he may grant you to be strength-ened with power through his Spirit in your in-ner being, so that Christ may dwell in your

hearts through faith—that you, being rooted and grounded in love, may have strength to comprehend with all the saints what is the breadth and length and height and depth, and to know the love of Christ that surpasses knowledge, that you may be filled with all the fullness of God. Now to him who is able to do far more abundantly than all that we ask or think, according to the power at work within us, to him be glory in the church and in Christ Jesus throughout all generations, forever and ever. Amen." (Ephesians 3:14-21 ESV)

Peter prayed for us:

"Grow in the grace and knowledge of our Lord and Savior Jesus Christ. To him be the glory both now and forever! Amen." (2 Peter 3:18 NKJV)

Jude prayed for us:

"To him who is able to keep you from stumbling and to present you before his glorious presence without fault and with great joy—to the only God our Savior be glory, majesty, power and authority, through Jesus Christ our Lord, before all ages, now and forevermore! Amen." (Jude 1:24-25 NIV)

May we always enjoy the pleasure of Our Father's company in prayer. May we always find our delight in Him whose name is "Majestic Glory" (2 Peter 1:17 ESV).

May we always walk hand in hand with Jesus our Savior – our brother – our friend – our King — our bridegroom – the One whose very name is Amen!

May we always be led by the Spirit as we search His Word to live more holy and righteous in the joy of His love.

May each day begin with praise and end with Amen! May our House of Prayer forever be filled with God's glory and praises that come from our sincere hearts.

May the words of our mouths and the meditations of our hearts always be . . .

"Amen!
Praise and glory and wisdom and thanksgiving
and honor and power and strength
be to our God for ever and ever.
Amen!"
Revelation 7:12 ESV

Prayer Guide
Outline

Copy or remove the Prayer Guide Outline
on the following page.
Keep it in your Bible or your Journal
as a reference and prayer prompter
when enjoying a time of prayer.

Prayer Guide Outline
The Pleasure of His Company

Jesus said, When you pray say,

OUR FATHER IN HEAVEN
Pause. Be still. Think about each word. Meditate upon my eternal family: Jesus my brother (Heb 2:11), my spiritual brothers and sisters who are the children of our Father (Mat 12:50; 1 Jn 3:1). Thank God for His family. See myself coming hand in hand with Jesus to the throne of Our Father, surrounded by angels (Ps 73:23-25, Heb 12:22-24)

HALLOWED BE YOUR NAME
Reaffirm to God that I will not misuse His name, but will speak it only with honor and respect (Ex 20:7, Ps 105:3). Think about God's names and praise Him for meeting my needs because of the blessing promised in each name. Encourage myself because the grace of Jesus, the love of the Father, and the fellowship of the Holy Spirit is with me (2 Cor 13:14).

YOUR KINGDOM COME
Open my mind to let Jesus take His rightful place as King of everything in my life (Ps 24:9, 1 Tim 1:17). Examine myself to be certain that I am seeking first His kingdom and righteousness (2 Cor 13:5, Mat 6:33-34). Rearrange my priorities as needed.

Think about Jesus my bridegroom (Is 62:5; Eph 5:25-27, 30; 2 Cor 1:1, 11:2; Rev 19:7-9). Encourage myself because nothing can separate me from Jesus (Rom 8:35-39, Mat 19:6).

YOUR WILL BE DONE ON EARTH AS IT IS IN HEAVEN
Pray: Teach me to do your will (Ps 143:10). Recommit to allow God to rule in my life (Ps 103:19, Lk 17:21), to praise, to do His bidding, to obey His word, to be His servant and do His will (Ps 103:21), to worship Jesus (Heb 1:6), to come together with the family of God in joyful assembly (Heb 12:22), to look carefully into the plan of salvation (1 Pet 1:12).

Pray for those who come to mind who are lost (Mat 18:14, 28:19-20; Lk 14:21,23; Jn 1:12-13). Pray for opportunities to be a servant of God's will (Phil 2:4,5,7; Gal 6:9-10).

GIVE US TODAY OUR DAILY BREAD
Present my requests to God (Phil 1:4-6, Jam 4:2-3). Meditate upon God's promises to meet my needs (Mat 7:7-11, Phil 4:19). Examine my motives (Jam 4:3). Ask God to guide me in my obedience to give (Mat 7:11-12; Lk 6:38).

Thank God for His words—my spiritual bread (Mat 4:4; Jn 6:32-35, 2 Tim 3:16-17). Nourish myself by reading the Bible.

Pray for people who have asked me to pray about their needs.

AND FORGIVE US OUR SINS
Think about seeing Jesus face-to-face (1 Th 4:16-17; Rev 22:20). Am I ready? Ask the Holy Spirit to reveal areas in my life that are not pleasing to God so that I can confess them and be free from their effects (Ps 19:12-13, 2 P 3:10-11, 14; Rev 3:19-20).

Visualize Jesus on the cross. See my sin placed on Him. Feel His love for me. With spiritual ears, hear Him say, "I forgive you!" (1 Jn 1:7-9) Apologize to anyone I have offended (Mat 5:23-25; Rom 13:7-10).

AS WE ALSO HAVE FORGIVEN THOSE WHO SINNED AGAINST US
Forgive others (Mat 6:14; Lk 6:37-38; Rom 13:7-10; Eph 4:31-32). Pray for repentance in the one who sinned against me (Rom 2:4b). Pray to be prepared for those who will sin against me in the future. Make up my mind to return good for evil (Mat 18:21-22; Rom 12:19-21). Pray for those who mistreat me (Lk 6:27-37; Mat 5:44). Ask God to increase my strength and resolve to love others (1 Cor 13:4-8).

LEAD US NOT INTO TEMPTATION
Watch for temptation from myself, my companions, and worldly desires (Jam 1:13-15; Gal 6:1; 1 Cor 15:33; 1 Jn 2:16-17). Claim God's promise not to let me be tempted beyond what I can bear (1 Cor 10:13). When tempted, pray for help finding God's promised way out (1 Cor 10:13). Remind myself that Jesus will help me (Heb 2:14,18; 4:15; 13:5b; 2 Cor 1:21).

Vow to honor God with my body (1 Cor 6:20), to flee from sexual immorality, greed, love of money, and evil desires (1 Cor 6:18, 10:14; Col 3:5; 1 Tim 6:6-10, 2 T 2:22). Vow to rid myself of anger, rage, malice, slander, filthy language, telling lies (Col 3:5-8).

BUT DELIVER US FROM THE EVIL ONE
Be self-controlled and alert for the devil's temptations (1 Pet 5:8-10). Resist the evil one (Jam 4:7-8). Put on God's armor of light (Rom 13:12,14, Eph 6:11-18):
> Belt of Truth (Jn 8:31-32, 14:6)
> Breastplate of Righteousness (2 Cor 5:21)
> Shoes of Readiness (Rom 10:15; Gal 5:25; 1 Jn 1:6)
> Shield of Faith (Heb 11:1,6, Ps 7:10, 28:7, 91:4)
> Helmet of Salvation (1 Th 5:8-9; Ps 140:7-8; Phil 4:7)
> Sword of the Spirit = Words of God (Eph 6:17-18; Jn 6:3; 1 Pet 1:13)

FOR YOURS IS THE KINGDOM,
AND THE POWER AND THE GLORY FOREVER
Praise God because He has invited me to be a participant with Him ...
> ... in His Kingdom (Col 1:13; 2 Tim 4:18; 1 Tim 1:17)
> ... in His Power (Isa 40:29-31; 1 Cor 6:14; Phil 4:13)
> ... in His Glory (Heb 1:3; 2 C 3:18, Heb 2:10; Rom 8:17-18; 1 Pet 5:10)
Meditate upon eternity (Heb 1:8, Ps 57:19; Rev 5:13)

IN JESUS NAME. AMEN.
Close my prayer in Jesus name, acknowledging Him as my intercessor (Jn 16:23-24; Heb 7:24-25). Say Jesus' name, "Amen." (Rev 3:14)

Also Available

Your personal prayer guide to go with

The Pleasure of His Company

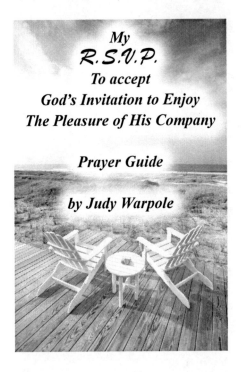

My
R.S.V.P.
To accept
God's Invitation to Enjoy
The Pleasure of His Company

Prayer Guide

by Judy Warpole

*My RSVP prayer guide follows the same themes as the chapters in **The Pleasure of His Company**. Each section is designed so that you read scripture, letting God speak to your mind and heart. Then, you will be instructed to pray in your own words or read the prayer that is shown. Soon you will get into the flow of a two-way spiritual conversation with God Our Father.*

https://judywarpole.com

CPSIA information can be obtained at www.ICGtesting.com
Printed in the USA
LVOW10s0107081013

355814LV00001B/1/P